MEMOIRS OF CYRIL JONES

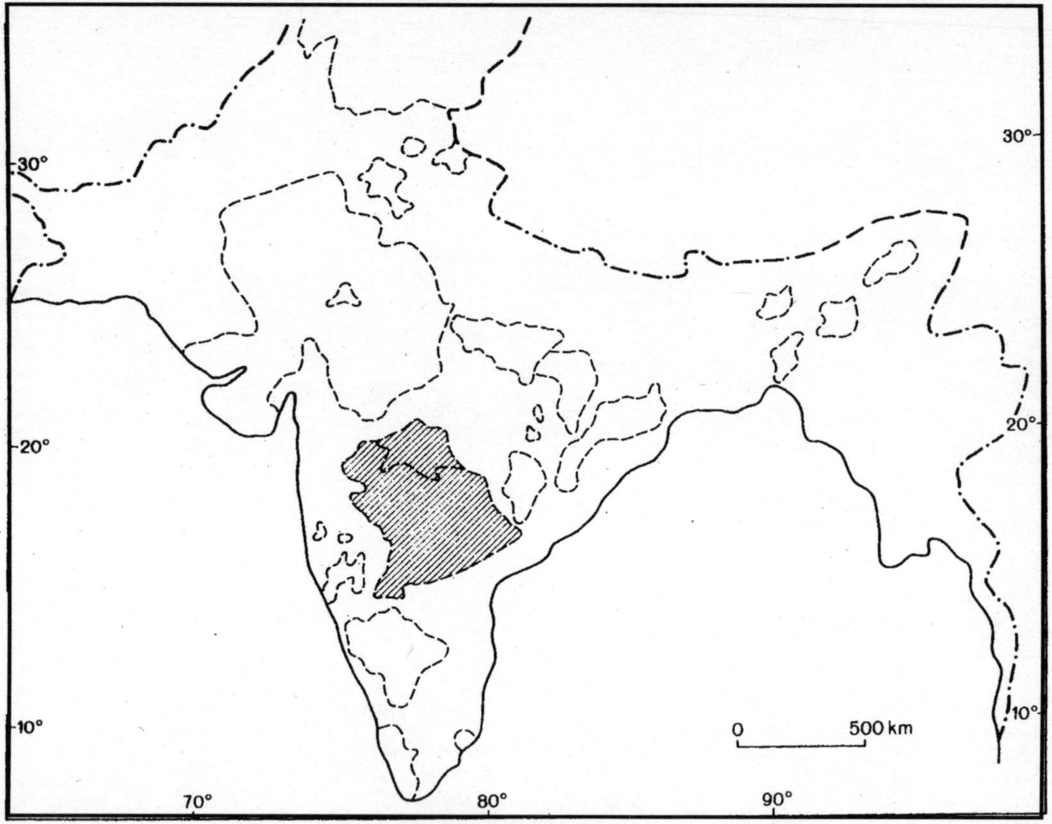

Hyderabad state in 1948

MEMOIRS OF CYRIL JONES

People, Society and Railways in Hyderabad

Edited by

OMAR KHALIDI

MANOHAR
2020

First published 1991
POD reprint 2020

ISBN 978-81-85425-54-2

Published by
Ajay Kumar Jain *for*
Manohar Publishers & Distributors
4753/23 Ansari Road, Daryaganj
New Delhi 110 002

Printed at
Replika Press Pvt. Ltd.

Preface

Hyderabad, Deccan under the Nizams (c.1720 – 1948) was the largest princely dominion in India. With its own army, postal service, currency, and communications system it had most of the attributes of a modern State in the making. This collection of essays, while primarily concerned with one component of communication system, namely the railways of the erstwhile state of Hyderabad, officially known as the Nizam's State Railways (N.S.R.), also provides insights into the social life of Hyderabad.

Y. Saraswati Rao provides a concise history of N.S.R., from its inception in the 1860s to its extinction in 1950. This is followed by an autobiographical account by Cyril Walter Lloyd Jones (1881–1981) the British railway engineer who had been closely associated with the N.S.R., edited by his grandson David Lloyd Jones. Writings by or about technical or managerial personnel of railways in India are few, and therefore Cyril Jones's record of his experience in Hyderabad is valuable for its rarity, if nothing else. In addition to the development of railways, his account provides us useful glimpses of the nobility, state officials, people and society of the Hyderabad state during the period of his stay. Finally, the editor of the volume has combed through various books and journals to produce a bibliographic essay that brings together what little has been written on the Nizam's State Railways.

The publication of the book was greatly assisted by Ghalib Ibn Awad Al–Quaiti of Hadramawt, for which he deserves my special thanks.

Omar Khalidi

Contents

List of Maps and Illustrations

Maps

Illustrations

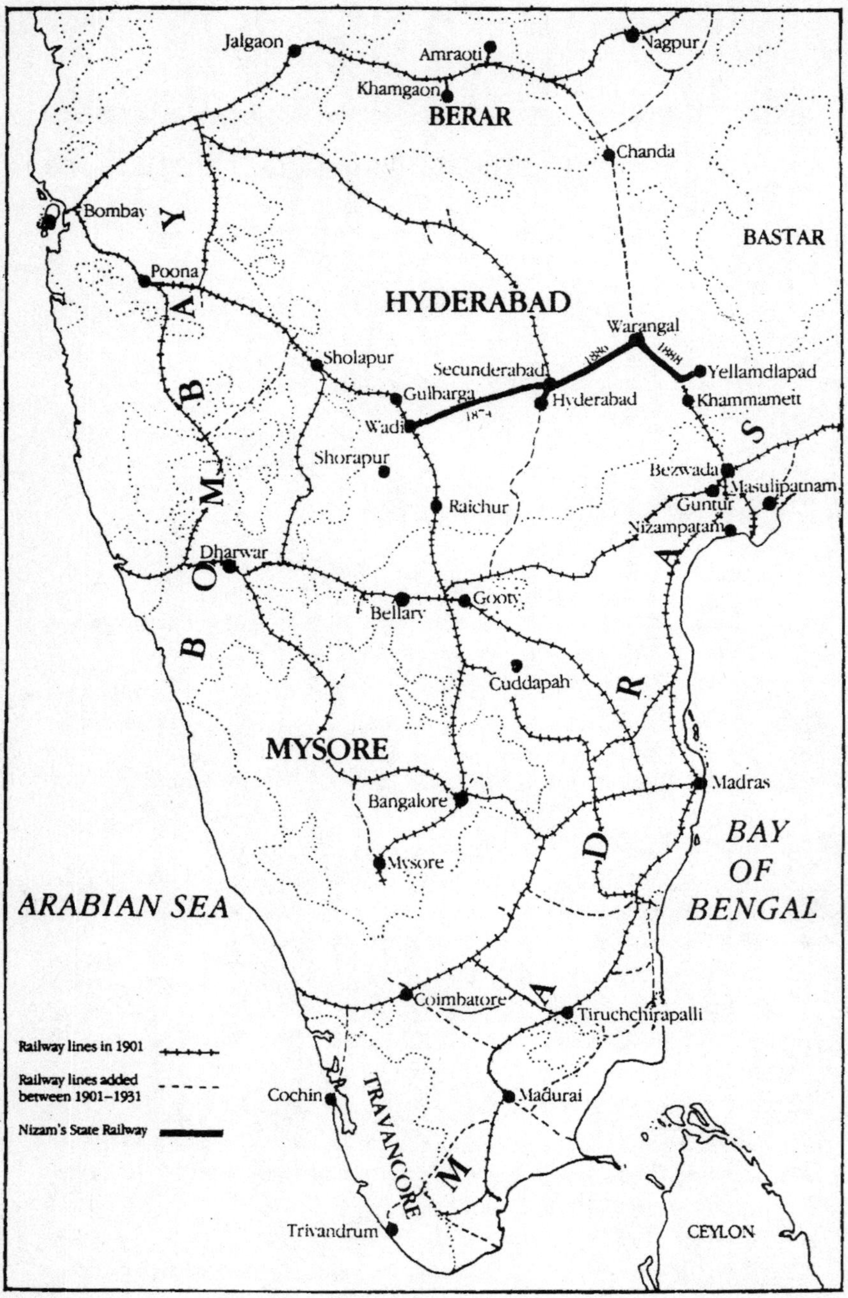

Railways in the Nizam's Dominion

I

Development of Nizam State Railways

Y. Sarasvati Rao

The State of Hyderabad was mainly agricultural in character, its principal products being grain, pulses, oil seeds, cotton and coal. The markets for its produce were, to a large extent, beyond the state boundaries and access to them was possible through connection with the neighbouring railway systems of the Great Indian Peninsular Railway (G.I.P.) and Madras and Southern Maratha (M & SM) Railway administrations. It is in this background that the development of the Nizam State Railway (N.S.R.) is to be viewed.

The earliest section of railway to be surveyed and constructed in the state was the Wadi-Secunderabad line. The survey began on 30th October, 1869 and construction on the 25th March, 1871. The government of H.H. the Nizam provided the capital and the Government of India constructed the line, which was opened for traffic on 9th October, 1874. Up to the end of 1878, the line was worked by the Great Indian Peninsular Railway Company (G.I.P.) with its own rolling stock. From January, 1879 to 31st December, 1884, it was worked by the State Railway Agency.

H.H. the Nizam, Mir Osman Ali Khan, was an year old prince when the first train arrived on the decorated platform of the Hyderabad railway station. The occasion was celebrated with pomp and glitter in the twin cities and it is reported that the tedious royal formalities were gone through with dignity and maturity by the young prince when he was presented the congratulatory message from the Viceroy of India.

Sir Salar Jung I had apportioned a million sterling of the State funds for construction of the State Railway by way of its total cost.

The British Government had its own reasons for encouraging the railway. The Bombay Government and the Resident at Hyderabad strongly recommended the formation of a rail road to the city of Hyderabad for military and political reasons. Hyderabad, they urged, was the largest military station in southern India. While Hyderabad was a better point for a railway to connect the east and west coasts and the south of the Peninsula of India, it had the gravest objection however, to a through line, on which military communications had to depend, passing close to and round the capital of a foreign state. In the case of an outbreak, the railway connection could be very easily cut off. The inhabitants of Hyderabad were known to be hostile to the British and there was much reason to anticipate internal commotion and changes in the condition of society in the city.

On 15th May, 1877, a deputation waited upon the Secretary of State for India, at the India Office, concerning the extension of railways in the territories of the Nizam of Hyderabad. This deputation consisted of gentlemen interested in Indian affairs, among whom were the Chairman and Director of the G.I.P. and M. & S.M. railway companies, Mr. Edmund Ashworth, Chairman of the Manchester Chamber of Commerce, and a number of members of the British Parliament. Mr Bright, in introducing the subject of discussion, spoke strongly in favour of the proposed railways and urged that no obstacles should be interposed to money being raised in England for such useful purposes. The M.Ps. and the Chairman of the Manchester Chamber of Commerce pointed out the immense advantages not only to the native states, but to India generally, that must result from the railways. Lord Salisbury, while commenting about the lack of response from the Government of India on this project, felt that the resources of the native states could be developed by the instrumentality of railways. The railways were to be extended as rapidly as possible.

The State Railway had considerable political and commercial importance. There was a large trade already between the Nizam's territory and that of the imperial Government. Cotton, sugar, oils and grains were largely exported, while Hyderabad imported English goods to the tune of £ 400,000 a year. These imports and exports were obviously expected to increase with the facilities afforded by the new railways and more rapid communication.

But the ruler of Hyderabad had other reasons in mind for starting the railways in the state. These reasons were focused more on his subjects and with an idea to enable proper all– round development. The building of the rail road was to be a great blessing providing employment to the poor, who at that time were almost dying of starvation from famine and cholera.

After the commencement of the very first railway line between Wadi and Secunderabad, sectional extension programmes started with the first section of extension from Secunderabad to Warangal which was opened for traffic on 8th April, 1986. As far as the construction of lines was concerned, the British Government was clever enough to lay down certain conditions which the Nizam's Government had no alternative but to accept. The compelling reasons were: first, the State Government had no expertise available in this new venture, and had to look for it in the neighbouring railways, viz., the G.I.P. Railways; second, the State of Hyderabad had commercial interests outside the State and railway transport would provide quick transit as well as better marketing facilities for their agricultural produce and mineral wealth, mainly coal. Third, the state was landlocked and its markets could only be reached by means of lines connecting it with the railway systems of the G.I.P. and the M. & S.M. which could afford access to such ports as Bombay, Madras, Kakinada, Marmagoa, Masulipatam and, also, to all other ports of India. It was therefore necessary for the Hyderabad government to have cordial understanding and proper rapport with these private railway companies, all of which had their controlling Boards in England.

On 29th February 1864, the English government was about to construct a rail road between Sholapur and Hyderabad. A despatch from the Duke of Argyll, laid down the principles on which the undertaking should be executed and managed. Active negotiations followed between the Hyderabad Resident, Mr. Saunders and Sir Salar Jung I. The Nizam's government was prepared to construct the lines as a state project or undertake financial partnership with the Government of India. The State Government was certain that the building of the railway would not be given out on contract. After detailed consideration and deliberation with the Hyderabad Resident, Major Meade, the Viceroy decided that the Chief Engineer of the P.W.D. (Public Works Department) under the Hyderabad Resident assisted by one or two experienced professional subordinates who were already surveying this project, should be entrusted with the project. The overall control would be that of the supreme government, P.W.D. The Nizam's engineers would have nothing to do with the work. "Not one of them, unless it might be the European principal of his Engineering college, would as yet be of any use in works of this kind." Sir Salar Jung met these arguments in full and with force.

In February 1870, Sir Salar Jung while sanctioning a line from Gulbarga to Hyderabad, invited contributions from the public. "All who wished well to Sirkar are asked to assist in providing the necessary capital." This, he said, could be done in two ways, either as a loan to the Nizam's government or by subscribing for shares. In the former case interest will be paid at the rate of 6% per annum, in the latter 5% will be guaranteed, besides a proportionate share of the net profits. The line will, of course, be constructed by English engineers, appointed by the Imperial Government, but they will be required to submit to the Sirkar a full account of income and outlay every six months. These accounts will also be laid before the British government, who will choose certain of the shareholders to examine and report upon them. The suggestions of these representatives will receive due consideration. However, a shareholder who wishes to dispose of his interest in the undertaking must first give notice of such desire to the Sirkar, which reserves to itself the power of granting or withholding permission to do so.

These statements of Sir Salar Jung indicate that the State was eager to enter into public business activity, by involving public financial participation. Nevertheless this share participation was aimed at developing the communication system within the state and not to encourage business speculations by moneyed people. Public participation is a normal feature in a popular democracy although rather rare under feudal governments.

The *Times of India* of the 10th June 1872, commented,

> "Very often in the dealings of our Supreme Rulers with native states, scant measure of justice and consideration is meted out to them, and thereby our true Imperial prestige is lowered. One illustration of this disposition cited was the apparently one sided arrangement with H. H. the Nizam regarding the Railway now under construction by the British P.W.D. in his Dominions for which, he has been made not only to give up all the required land to British jurisdiction in perpetuity, but also to provide all the capital and guarantee all the interest".

In 1881, Sir Diler Jung, Secretary to the government of the Nizam in the Home Department (Railways) for railway extensions, originated and formulated a scheme which had for its object the development of the resources of the Nizam's Dominions and was submitted to Sir Salar Jung with a memorandum dated 7th November 1881. There were two distinct proposals in this scheme–one for the purchase of the State railway and the construction of the extensions by the company and the other, the concession of all mining rights in the Dominions to that company.

Negotiations lasting a period of two years resulted in the formation of a company to carry out the railway part of the scheme with a share capital of 2 million and a debenture capital of another 2 million. The deed of agreement between the Government and the railway company was signed on the 27th December, 1883.

The object of formation of the company was that it should purchase the existing State Railway from Wadi to Secunderabad (at a cost of £ 1,666,666) and construct a single line of Railway about 210 miles in length from Secunderabad to Wadi and thence to the southern frontier towards Bezawada, at a total cost of 3 million and that it should also construct a second extension of about 160 miles in length from Warangal to the northern frontier to Chanda at a cost of the balance of capital of one million sterling.

It was pointed out in a memorandum on the railways budget estimate for 1297 Fasli, that if the State Railway had not been purchased by the company, the government would have had to spend an enormous sum of Rs. 43,20,000.00 in twenty years on the renewal of permanent way alone, which at the time the line was made over to the company, was in an unsatisfactory condition generally.

Thus came into existence, the H. H. the Nizam's Guaranteed State Railway Company in 1883. The government of H.H. the Nizam-ul-Mulk, Sovereign of the Hyderabad State through his accredited Representative, the Sardar Diler Jung Bahadur, while transferring the railways to the company, entered into agreement on certain control measures by the government. Some of them are:

(a) The government to have an inspecting officer to check the lines and rolling stock, to ensure public safety.
(b) Rates and fares as prevailing on the G.I.P. Railway.
(c) The company to carry the mail-bags for the postal department free of cost.
(d) The company to run at least one train both ways except when there is an accident or natural calamity.
(e) Company to carry troops of both H.H. the Nizam and the Government of India.

In a nutshell, all the inspecting and regulatory functions which the Government of India was doing on other company railways in the country were done by the Nizam's government in the case of the Nizam's Government State Railway Company. However, the inspecting officer was to be appointed in consultation with and approval of the Government of India i.e. The British government.

The new railway company had the following composition of Directors:

Sir John Strachy, the Finance Minister of India	-	Chairman
Major General Sir Richard John Meade, K.C.S.I. British Resident in Hyderabad	-	Director
Lt. General- Alexander Fraser, Secretary, P.W.D. Government of India	-	Director
A.R. Schoble, Director G.I.P. Railway Company	-	Director
John Stewart, Director, National Provincial Bank of England, Ltd.	-	Director
John Cleghorn, Director North Eastern Railway Company	-	Director
O.C. Waterfield, Director, Imperial Ottoman	-	Director
Sirdar Diler Jung Bahadur, Secretary to the Nizam's Government Railway department	-	Director
A.M. Rendel, Consulting Engineer for State Railways to Her Majesty's Secretary of State of India	- -	Consulting Engineer
George H.M. Balten, Late Revenue Secretary to the Government of India	-	Secretary

One thing that is significant and which cannot be overlooked while glancing at the composition of the Board of Directors, is that care was taken to establish a rapport between the Government of India, the British Resident in Hyderabad, the bankers in England, the neighbouring railway companies like G.I.P. Railway as well as a remote railway company like North Eastern Railway Company. The Nizam's government Representative dealing with railway matters, the consulting engineer appointed in consultation with the Government of India, who, in fact, was already a consulting engineer to the British Ruler's Secretary of State of India, as well as the previous Revenue Secretary to the Government of India. The idea could have been that this new railway company should have arrangements through its composition, for an interplay of definite and authentic relevant experiences and knowledge in overall policy starting with the British crown through the Secretary of State of India and his consulting engineer's policy within the country through the Finance Minister of India, Secretary, Public Works Department, Government of India, and the Revenue Secretary to the Government of India; railway policy and its technical requirements from the point of view of technical uniformity within the country through the involvement of G.I.P. Railway and the North Eastern Railways and within the State through the British Resident in Hyderabad and the official Director, Sirdar Diler Jung Bahadur Secretary to the Nizam's Government, Railway Department. Thus a simple arrangement was made within the Board of Directors to have a direct chain of British Governments' intentions on railway matters in the State of Hyderabad from England to the city of Hyderabad. As far as the bankers were concerned, they had their guaranteed interest etc., a financial agreement but otherwise, the scheme was to be operated as per the desire of the British government, within the dominions of the Nizam.

These impressions are gained from the fact that Sir George Yule, who had been Resident in the Court of the Nizam earlier and who was to represent the shareholders now, was quite pessimistic about the purchase of State Railways by the company and expressed his apprehensions in his letter to the editor of *The Times* (London) published on 31st December, 1883. He, being familiar with the resources of the Nizam then, opined, "the resources of Hyderabad State are unequal to the burden of £ 2,00,000 per annum, proposed to be laid upon it, and that sooner or later, the shareholders must be prepared for a failure of income." But there was also a different view that the construction of this railway was of immense strategic importance to the British government and it was consequently being forced regardless of the wishes of the Nizam's council and the Nizam himself, who was within three months of attaining his majority, and whose first act might be to repudiate all responsibility for this engagement. Protracted exchange of this kind of correspondence took place but the company was ultimately formed. The company worked all the sections from January, 1885 to 31st March, 1930.

In 1903, the Special Commission for Railways, asked Thomas Robertson to report on the administration and working of the Indian railways. Management of railways in the state did not come within direct purview of this Commission for obvious reasons except that from the point of view of the safety of the travelling public, the maintenance of the track and the rolling stock, it had to be periodically inspected by an agency outside the state, since all trains passed through the territory of the Nizam. Therefore, the Commission made a mention of this point. Besides, the Indian Railway Act of 1890 provided for overall supervisory control over state railways by virtue of an arrangement with the Indian states. In 1920-1921, another Committee under the chairmanship of Sir William Ashworth made an overall revision of the Indian railway system mainly from the financial point of view and in that context commented on the administration also. This Committee recommended some sort of an all India railway policy as well as a review from a broad standpoint, and better relations between the railways belonging to the Government of India and the other state railways.

The committee also had a favourable comment to make on the N.G.S. Railway Company, with regard to the Indianization of the superior level personnel. The percentage of Indians in the N.G.S.R. was 15.25% as against other railways in the country and particularly the immediate neighbour, the G.I.P. Railway which registered a figure as low as five per cent.

A significant observation made by the Ashworth Committee was about the Boards having absentee control over the Indian railway managements. The Committee felt that the London Boards were advantageous for expert and technical knowledge possessed by many of the Directors.

> "But conditions in India have changed so greatly in the last few years and are changing so rapidly at this moment, that whatever may have been the position in the past, we think the advantages of English management are now outweighed by the great disadvantages of absentee control and the difficulty of keeping in close touch with the modern social and trade conditions of India."

While constituting the N.G.S. Railway Company, the contracts entitled the government to acquire the railway undertaking on 1st January, 1914, 1934 and 1954. This right was not exercised in 1914 but the government intended to exercise it in 1934. Therefore in 1929, a retired Auditor General to the Government of India, Sir Fredric Gauntlett was asked to study the proposed acquisition of the railways owned by H.H., the Nizam's G.S. Railway Co. Ltd., by the Nizam's government. While presenting his report, Sir Fredric supported the recommendations made by Sir Freeman with regard to the management authority. Sir Freeman, one of the foremost railway experts in England was asked to advise the government among other matters on the management of the railways by the state, the development of the system by construction of new lines to meet future demands and matters of interest to the state as owners of the railways responsible for their success as a commercial undertaking and for serving the needs of the community.

Sir Freeman seems to have been influenced by two facts. While the main recommendations of the management of the Nizam State Railways was to be entrusted to a Board, all other details seem to have flowed from these basic recommendations. The two facts could have been, the Government of India had constituted a Railway Board in 1905, through an act and the guaranteed company also had a Board system of management. Therefore, the logical outcome a was Board for the Nizam State Railway also. His detailed recommendations about the Board were:

Location of the Board

(a) The Headquarters of the Board was to be in London.
(b) One of the members, (preferably two) should visit the undertaking every year.
(c) A full report of every meeting of the Board should be sent to the government, through the finance member, and
(d) The Agent should keep the Board informed of any discussions he may have with the government.

The most important work of the Board would be performed during the annual visit. The budget would be passed, questions of policy and capital programmes would be discussed with the government, the efficiency of the administration of the undertaking would be tested on the spot and all proposals for enhancing the values of the undertaking as a commercial concern would be discussed by the Agent.

Strength of Board

This should depend on the quality and not on the number of individual members. The number should be kept at the minimum which will supply all the qualifications needed. Usually this would be four in addition to the

Finance Member. The Chairman should have a recognised status in Indian affairs. Two members should have practical experience of railway administration (one of whom at least must have Indian experience) and one should have experience of state, while one member at least, in addition to the Finance Member, should have financial experience.

Tenure of Office

While all the members would be liable for removal at the government's will, it was essential for the efficient working of the Board that in practice, they should be assured of some continuity of office. Therefore, one member was to be replaced each year so that in ordinary circumstances, a member would serve for at least five years.

It was Sir Freeman who recommended the beginning of a road transport system under the railway administration to avoid unhealthy competition between railways and roadways and at the same time to bring about rail-road co-ordination. It was a convenient method to direct the profits accruing in road transport to the railways.

In deference to the recommendations of the two experts, the management of the N.S. Railway was entrusted to a Board which consisted of the Finance Member as the ex-officio President and four other members, one of whom was to be the Chairman in London in the absence of the President and another the Managing Director. The Finance Member was the representative of the Executive Council on the Board and the representative of the Board on the Council and had authority to have a full and free exchange of views with the Agent in India and the Members of the Board in London. The Board was to meet part of the year in Hyderabad and part of the year in London.

On 1st April, 1930, the Government acquired all the property and assets of the N.G.S.R. Co. other than their reserve and undertook all their liabilities, other than those relating to their stock and debenture holdings. Thenceforth, the railway owned and operated by the government was known as H.H. Nizam's State Railway. To cope with the increased work developing upon the Railway Department, in consequence of the government policy for steady expansion of the railway system, the work of the traffic department under the traffic manager was bifurcated into two branches, viz., Commerce and Transportation with a separate head for each.

The Chairman and the Managing Director of the State Railway Board were both stationed in London, being Englishmen and visited Hyderabad periodically to hold meetings and discuss "important subjects like capital and revenue estimates." In India (i.e. in Hyderabad) H.H. the Nizam's nominee was an official Director as well as the local President for the Board Meetings. An Englishman was the Agent of the London based Board as well as the Chief Engineer. This arrangement in the unusual composition of the Board of a state government railway which ought to have had all members from the dominions of the Nizam, seems to have been for the following reasons:-

1. The future construction of the railways as part of the expansion programme also should be as per the standards of the All India Railways and such a standard could have been expected only through a British Engineer. This had been a condition earlier too, when the state had started its railway project.
2. In the financial settlement with the N.G.S.R. Co, at the time of the company takeover the agreement with regard to payment was that part of it was to be made in cash (i.e. 1½ million sterling) and the balance through the issue of three year debentures carrying interest at 5½%, as well as shares. For the cash payment, government obtained accommodation at approximately 6% from the Imperial Bank of India. All this only went to prove the financial unsoundness of the government of the state of Hyderabad, which was to shoulder such huge liabilities and yet for various other reasons had decided to take over the railways. But the Company and the British rulers of the country who were more concerned about the Company's financial interest, arranged to have the State Railway Board to operate from London and they themselves occupied key positions on the Board. The State Government could be easily convinced of the usefulness of this arrangement under the guise of railway expertise being available with the English, etc.
3. From the viewpoint of the State Government perhaps it was necessary to manage the State Railways with the expert guidance and help of the English experts who were already managing the State Railways through the Company. The takeover was to be manoevoured gradually and not suddenly, so that some sort of continuity could be ensured in the programmes.

This kind of arrangement in the composition of the Board as well as the location of the Board continued for about a decade. During this decade, except the President who was a representative of H.H. the Nizam and a local nobleman, all others were Englishmen i.e., both policy-makers as well as the Chief Engineer.

However, when the Second World War broke out, it was difficult to manage the State Railway from London. Therefore, on 1st November, 1941, the Nizam State Railway Board was shifted from London to Hyderabad, although a London Agent remained to represent the railway interests from there.

As a result of the Federal Financial integration with effect from 31st April, 1950, the N.S. Railway became part of the central government.

From the State's point of view, its railway system was a public utility undertaking and formed a vital part of the economic and social structures of the State. The maintenance of this system in a state of efficiency and its development and extension from time to time to meet the growing needs of the inhabitants of the State, were matters of paramount importance.

The railway system was maintained in a high state of efficiency and in a sound economic condition earning a good return upon the capital which it represented.

The policy of the Nizam's Railway for extensions was very clear i.e.:

(1) The most remunerative route was to be selected which meant that a line through traffic would be most paying.
(2) If obtaining such a traffic was possible by connecting their railway with other railways, then extension with this object was to be made.
(3) If outside traffic was not advantageous, the consideration would be to see what could be done for local traffic and find out which lines will best open up productive and populous part of the State.
(4) Alternatively, any local development of the State which would give large through traffic.
(5) Finally consider which line would tend most to the development of the internal resources of the country.

In formulating the railway policy, besides the above five considerations, the guarantee of H.H.'s Government to meet all needs from revenue coming from the Nizam's subjects must be kept in mind. It was due to them that the public revenue should be used to their benefit. It had been reiterated that for the reason of material prosperity of the people and the increase of the revenue, a new line may be constructed which would improve internal communication.

Some Unique Features of the N.S. Railway Administration

1. Railway administration was made in charge of road transport also, so

that while rail-road coordination could be easily achieved, the drop in earnings in railways could be made good through the road transport system. To make this an effective arrangement a rail-road service was introduced for goods and a common rail-cum-bus ticket, was introduced for passengers, in the year 1933.

2. N.S. Railway was operating the airways also under a firman issued by H.H. the Nizam in 1938.

3. Indianization had been gradually arranged at the executive and operational level, but the Board continued to be controlled by the English.

4. The general multi-religious composition of the Nizam's subjects was well represented in the railway service as is seen from documented evidence in the General Manager's annual reports:

STATUTORY INDIANS IN THE N.S. RAILWAY SERVICE

	Europeans	Hindus	Muslims	Anglo-Indians	Sikhs	Indian Christians	Others
1935	75	12,601	2,446	416	9	703	58
1936	75	12,162	2,211	346	6	658	33

REFERENCES

1. Hundred years of Indian Railways 1853-1953.
2. Nizam's Administration Reports.
3. Reports on Indian Railways.
4. History of Indian Railways. New Delhi Railway Board, 1958.
5. Robertson Committee Report 1903 on Indian Railways.
6. Ashworth Committee Report on Indian Railways 1920.
7. Various Documented printed material from 1883 to 1950.
8. Reports on the working of H.H. the Nizam's Guaranteed State Railway Co., 1886-1887.
9. General Manager's Annual Reports of the Nizam State Railway 1938, 1940, 41, 1939, 1929-30 to 1935-36, 1920.
10. Sir Frederic Gauntlett Report-1929.
11. Sir Freemen's Report.
12. Hyderabad Affairs-1864 onwards.
13. N.S. Railway Report from 1874-1895 by Sardar Dilerul-Mulk Bahadur.

II

Cyril Walter Lloyd Jones: A Railway Engineer in Hyderabad

David Lloyd Jones

Early Life

A long standing dispute in the family revolved around where Cyril Walter Lloyd Jones was born. He strongly maintained that it was St Leonards-on-Sea, whereas his mother, who might be thought to know better, always said that her eldest son and second child had been born in London. The truth was finally established beyond cavil when the birth certificate was obtained to satisfy the Queen's Secretary that he had reached his hundredth year. Wandsworth had the distinction of being his birthplace. The confusion seems to have arisen on account of the family having moved to the coast from London shortly after Cyril's birth and he was, in fact, christened in St Leonards.

On 6th March 1881 (the date of Cyril's birth) Gladstone had formed his second ministry and the first Boer War had broken out. Queen Victoria had a further twenty years to reign. The power of Britain and the glory of her Empire were at their zenith. When Cyril died on 10th July 1981, the picture had very markedly changed. Yet as he used to say in later life, no man could have lived through a more exciting period of change, of advance in knowledge and of material development. Born at the time he was, he was in a position to take advantage of the enormous vista of opportunity open before him. He was fortunate indeed to avoid the worst disasters of the century and his abilities and energy enabled him to benefit from the progress of the age.

Something of the family history has been supplied by Cyril's nephew, Leonard Read. In about 1820, John Jones ran a small woollen mill at Cwmbran near Llanidloes in Central Wales. The stone building still stands on the corner of the road leading to Tylwch station but has now been converted to a joinery shop. He had no less than twelve children of whom Mary was the eldest and Richard the youngest. On the death of his wife, who had produced this tribe, John decided to marry again and this offended his children. They must have been of a rebellious nature as some of the members had been involved in the Chartist Movement. At any rate, led by Mary, the family decided to break with their father and emigrate to the United States. They settled in Scranton, Pennsylvania, where on the whole they prospered as coal owners. Contact has been maintained between the descendants of those emigrants and the Lloyd Jones family to this day and we still address each other as cousins.

Too young to go with his brothers and sisters, Richard the youngest, stayed back with his father and was apprenticed to a saddler in Ludlow. This arrangement seems to have been arrived at in lieu of repayment of a debt owed to John Jones rather than any decision on the merits of the trade. After completing his indenture, Richard moved to Shaftsbury and set up a saddlers shop. This was not a success and he moved on to Market Harborough to try again. There he met and married Mary Heath, a girl who had been brought up by an aunt and about whose parentage a romantic mystery clings, which to elaborate on would take us beyond the scope of this narrative. Four children resulted from this marriage of whom Richard (junior) born in 1852, was the eldest. The Market Harborough business also failed and the family moved to the Holloway district in London where persistence was finally rewarded.

Richard junior worked for his father and in course of time, married Louisa Keel. Her father had suffered a business failure when his partner absconded with the joint assets. Whether it was because of this or from a low opinion of Louisa's suitability as a wife, it is not clear but Richard's parents disapproved of the match. Moreover, father and son were frequently in conflict, both suffering from a family trait of a quick temper. The children of this marriage were Edith, born in 1878, Cyril, Richard Llewellyn (Dick), Leonard and Harold. Leonard died when he was four. Parting from his father, Richard junior managed a shop in Wandsworth for a time and then started a harness factory which prospered to an extent that he was able to sell it out at a considerable profit.

The family moved to Finchley where Cyril along with his sister attended his first school.

Richard was never content to remain in the same job for long and his restlessness now took him overseas. Quite unrelated to any previous work that he had done, he was engaged as the manager of a coffee plantation in East Africa. He left his family behind and on returning to England they all moved to Wood Green. He next tried his hand as a mining surveyor in the Gold Coast. This too did not last long and next he set up a saddlery business and livery stable in Southampton. A dishonest manager caused the collapse of this business and the family returned to Wood Green and Richard tried his hand once more in the Gold Coast. Ravaged by malaria, he was forced to remain in England for sometime. He had previously been approached by his American cousins to join them and this he finally did but again leaving the family behind. He worked as a coal mine manager in Virginia but was dissatisfied with the work and intended to abandon it when he died in 1904.

The family wanderings do not seem to have disturbed Cyril's upbringing. His father being frequently absent, his mother was the main influence. As was normal in those times and with the added reinforcement of a Welsh background, religion played a powerful part in the boy's development. The style of life was middle class at a moderate level of comfort but with never too much money to spare. After junior school, Cyril went to the Haberdasher Askes School in London. There he showed promise in mathematics and science and impressed his form master to the extent that he persuaded the school governors to provide Cyril with a scholarship to the Central Technical College in London.

The years at the Central, which later became the Imperial College of Science, were the most important in shaping the young engineer. He encountered the full impact of modern scientific teaching, which with his natural bent towards mathematics, provided the basis for all his future working methods. It became his unvarying practice to apply mathematical analysis to all problems confronting him and to arrive at solutions ahead of those being used by the bulk of engineers. More than that, the reasoned logic of his mind was of the greatest value in dealing with administrative matters outside the field of engineering.

It was while he was at the Central, that he made friendships that were to last him through life. Ralph Freeman, his closest and most enduring friend was later partner in the firm of Freeman Fox, Consulting Engineers, who amongst much else designed the Sidney Harbour Bridge. Edwin Culley was another friend who was later the editor of an engineering journal.

For the period immediately after leaving the Central, it would be best to give Cyril Lloyd Jones' own account, as he wrote it down many years later.

"In September 1899, having completed my course at the Central, I called on Professor Unwin hoping that he would suggest how I could get employment. He said that one of his old students, Gibbs, had just left him and that he could employ a man at his factory at York. I joined Gibbs at York but after a few months it became clear that the job offered no experience and no prospects. Answering an advertisement, I then joined the drawing office of Piersons, a constructional steelwork firm in London and was soon not only obtaining valuable experience but acquiring an interest in the theory of elasticity, which has always remained. I was loth to leave Piersons but I did not want to be just a specialist in one branch of work and therefore I gladly accepted an invitation from my friend, Edwin Culley, to join him on a survey.

We spent a very happy summer of 1901 surveying and preparing the parliamentary plans for a light railway from Maidstone to Chatham. On completion of the work, Mertz and Maclellan, for whom we were working, asked me to go to Newcastle to work on designs of power stations. I spent the winter in Newcastle but it was not new experience, so I wrote to the Institute of Civil Engineers and at their suggestion joined Heathcote, a firm of architects in Manchester, as their engineer. Admittedly the pay was part of the attraction, £ 25 a month, high pay in those days for a man of twenty two, but there was some useful work in steel frames, foundations and building construction. But I had no inclination to cash in on my ability. I was determined to get more experience, and construction experience, if possible.

All my attempts were fruitless. Even my father, who was in Virginia and could have exercised influence, advised me to remain in England. Culley had joined me in the firm in Manchester and I had several other engineer assistants. One of these men who had recently come from India, was dining with me one day when I mentioned my ambitions and he advised me to try the Nizam's Railway. I had never considered India as a field for my activities because I had thought it reserved for Cooper's Hill and Chatham. However, I was offered the post of Assistant Engineer on the Nizam's Railway on Rs 350 to Rs 500 per month, the starting pay being about £ 20 a year less than I was drawing in England.

Looking back, I do not think that these three years in England were wasted but my real achievement was in York, where I met Kathleen Penty, aged sixteen, whom I married seven years later. During the three years before I left for India, I had always had one object in mind and that was to gain experience and particularly executive experience in construction. I had been made several financially attractive offers both in London and Manchester but they did not tempt me for a minute because they did not offer the work I wanted. It was very difficult to get what I wanted. The normal entry in civil engineering was as an articled pupil and entrants usually had some string pulling done for them. An academic training was almost a disadvantage. Thus my satisfaction at the Indian appointment was complete.

I must admit, however, that this was not the whole story. I had enjoyed the first three years of the century but it was not all I wanted from life. I cannot remember much of my spare time occupation in London but wherever I happened to be, theatres and dances occupied my evenings. In and around Manchester, I cycled quite a lot and also motored in the firm's 6 h.p. De Dion car with one of the partners, a considerable adventure in those days. The most joyful part of the three years, was the summer I spent with Culley surveying in Kent and I think that this experience must have reinforced an inherent desire for a life away from big cities. The appointment to India gave me my heart's desire and no happier man could have set sail, looking forward to the life and work abroad. My father was all against it and he came back to England to induce me to change my plans but soon realized that I was determined. He then gave me his gun, rifle and saddle as well as his theodolite and level and returned to the U.S.A. before I sailed.

Here was a young man full of enthusiasm and energy with confidence in his own abilities. He had no hesitation in changing jobs when he thought that he should broaden his experience. Moreover, he placed this above monetary reward. It is interesting to note, however, the apparent lack of appreciation among engineering firms for a man with good academic qualifications. The prevailing hidebound attitude valued an apprenticeship above mere book learning. Even so, he had no trouble in finding employment and his merits must have been well regarded for the Manchester firm to have paid him £ 300 a year.

The meeting in York with the girl who was to become his wife needs some elaboration. Kathleen Penty was the daughter of Frank Penty who worked at the headquarters of the London and North Eastern Railway. He was a man of some local prominence being a sidesman at the Minster and a hospital governor. They lived in a pleasant terrace house close to the River Ouse. Kathleen was the second oldest of a family of six girls and two boys. They all had a sound education in the local schools and went on to obtain vocational qualifications. Kathleen took up art and for a time studied at the Slade. As was normal in large Victorian families, the older children had the duty of looking after the younger ones.

Cyril always maintained that from his first meeting with Kathleen at a dancing class in York, the question of who he was going to marry was settled. Kathleen at sixteen could not be expected to be so definite but her suitor was a handsome young man who obviously had a future. It is not surprising that she was strongly influenced though she would have to wait a long time, and most of that time separated from her fiancé, before she could expect to marry.

The decision to seek a career in India is to some extent surprising. The family had no previous connection with India, although, as has previously been said, Richard Jones spent much time in Africa. It should be explained here that while the latter was abroad, he embellished his surname to Lloyd-Jones. His full name was Richard Llewellyn Jones and he came to signing his name R. Ll-Jones and this was taken by some to stand for Lloyd-Jones which Richard duly accepted. The Welsh with their paucity of surnames, which are, of course, only really first names, often have to resort to this method of distinction. Cyril seems to have used the double barrelled name from early on and in this narrative the bare surname will be henceforth used which was, in fact, the custom at the time.

In going to India, he was considering the work he was going to do and not the country. He was still anxious for wider engineering experience and it was his intention that just as he had done already, when he had learnt all that there was to know on the Indian railways, he would move on. In addition, as he has said, he was attracted to an open air life with the spice of adventure and India at that time was a name to conjure with, the jewel on the crown of the Empire. This, however, was not the opinion of his father who rated engineering in India low and claimed that engineers in India were held in poor esteem in other parts of the world. It would probably be true that overseas experience, and not only of India, would carry little weight in seeking employment back in the U.K. Another factor which influenced him was the low salary that he considered was being offered to his son. Nonetheless, determination was a powerful part of Cyril's character and once he had made up his mind, his father's advice was ineffective.

Kitting out for India was an elaborate and expensive business. His not very large financial reserves were soon exhausted and he had to obtain an advance of £ 50 from his mother, which she was to recoup from his last employer for whom he had written a 'section book' for which the money was still owing. As was the experience of many young men going out East for the first time, much of the equipment and clothing which unscrupulous outfitters foisted on him proved to be useless or out of fashion, whereas other things he should have had, he lacked. Not having lived in the country as opposed to the town and as a sign of the changing age, when it was more customary to ride a bicycle rather than a horse, he had to take a course of riding lessons.

So in April 1904 the young man, seen off by a group of friends, left from Farington Street station on route for Tilbury to board the P & O liner, *S.S. Britannia*. The voyage to India is described in his own words.

> "I made this voyage in an aura of romance and adventure I have never forgotten and I suppose it is an experience that could not happen now. Since then, sixty years of technical development have put all the world on our doorstep and made it familiar to us on the screen. But it was not so in the spring of 1904 when I saw places I had only read about and which took days and even weeks to reach. For years to come, I should be living a new and strange way of life. Gibraltar charmed me because the streets were full of people riding beautiful little Arab horses. Istambul was most impressive and I did not go to bed the night we passed it. I rose early to see the pilot take us into Port Said. I was travelling second class in a five berth cabin with four young men about my own age. I became friendly with one lad, Cobbet, who was being sent to Australia because it was thought that there would be more room for him there. The food was quite good but I did not like a heavy meal in the middle of the day and a sort of high tea about six. After we left Suez, we started *pull punkahs* in the dining room and sleeping on deck at night. I do not think I ever travelled on another ship with *pull punkahs* but passengers continued to sleep on deck in the twenties. The *Britannia* was bound for Australia and did not call at Bombay, so the Indian passengers transshipped to the *Peninsular* at Aden but there was no time to land. I made new friends on the *Peninsular* among the young men going out for the first time, mostly to join regiments, but a number of the older passengers took an interest in us. In later years, I often felt grateful to these older men for the trouble they

> took to try to influence our behaviour to Indians although at the time, I am afraid, I felt that I needed no tuition. Their general theme was that Indians had very good manners themselves and were quick to detect a lack of good form, so we would be letting the side down if we misbehaved. The passenger classes were divided longitudinally on the *Peninsular;* the second class had the starboard side, which seemed to me very unfair. As we were coming out in the middle of the hot weather, there were very few women and many young men on board and urged on by the older men our games were very energetic. At last one morning we dropped anchor in Bombay harbour."

The point about the starboard cabins on the way out was that they received the full force of the sun during the day and hence were infernally hot. This is thought to be the origin of the word 'posh' port - out - starboard - home.

First Years in India

"We landed by tender and my close friends of the last ten days dispersed and I heard no word of any of them again. I think what impressed me first about Bombay was the low cost of the *ticca-gharris* in which you could drive about all day for only a few pence. I was next impressed by the newly opened Taj Mahal Hotel, lit by its own generating plant in a small power house in front of it. The street scenes were more or less what I had been led to expect, so although they charmed me they did not surprise me. My surprise was to find the Army and Navy Stores and an efficient hotel like the Taj. The Nizam's Railway had English agents at Bombay on whom I called. It did not strike me at the time but I now think they might have given me some kind of welcome or advice. All they did was to give a railway pass and tell me that the train left at 21.00 hours. One result was that, as nobody had warned me that in India everyone travelled with their own bedding, I boarded the train without even a cushion and no washing things – for a twenty–four hour journey through the plains in the hot weather. Luckily, some English soldiers in the next compartment took pity on me and loaned me what they could. It was the railway which really introduced me to the India which was to adopt me. I can still remember the impact of Victoria Terminus in Bombay. The platform was all that Kipling had described and I felt like looking round for Kim among the crowd of passengers. It came as a shock because I had never realized that what Kipling described was still going on. Even the soldiers that befriended me seemed to be Kipling's soldiers when they gave me their idea of Hyderabad. We were in a four wheel `compo' of two compartments with a dividing door; I was in the first class side and they were in the second class compartment."

It is advisable to provide some description of the part of India where Lloyd Jones was to spend his whole career. Hyderabad lies in the centre of the peninsula, slightly to the south of the median point of the subcontinent. It was the largest of the Indian states, autonomous areas surrounded by British territory. Previously it had formed a province of the Moghul Empire but as the power of the latter waned, it had asserted its independence under rulers called Nizams. When various European countries began to encroach into India during the eighteenth century, Hyderabad at first sided with the French but as it became apparent who was going to come out on top, the Nizam judiciously changed sides. From that time onwards, Hyderabad remained closely wedded to the British cause, so much so that it obtained the sobriquet of 'faithful ally of the British' and the Nizam was honoured with the unique title of 'His Exalted Highness' and ranked first among the Indian Princes. As with all other such states in India, the ruler had full powers over internal affairs, but his relations with the outside world were controlled by the Government of India and a British representative, the Resident, kept a watchful eye to prevent more glaring abuses. In the case of Hyderabad, its finances had gone sadly awry and the Government of India imposed one of its officers as Finance Minister in the Nizam's Government. Despite the Nizam's loyalty to the British, his State has now ceased to exist as such. After a brief and futile struggle, when India gained Independence, it was dismembered and absorbed in the rest of the country.

Adjoining Hyderabad city was an enclave of British territory, Secunderabad. It included a military cantonment at Bolarum and the railway colony at Lalaguda. Typical of a larger 'station' in British India it was a spaciously laid out residential area with tree lined avenues between whitewashed bungalows set in large gardens. A club, a church and shops selling European goods provided the necessary amenities. At a reasonable altitude, it also avoided the extremes of hot weather and was generally considered to be one of the better stations both for the military and civil life. It was here that the newcomer Cyril Lloyd Jones arrived and he goes on to describe it.

"The train arrived at Secunderabad about five in the afternoon and I was met by a genial old gentleman, C.B. Dunlop, the Chief Engineer. I do not understand why he came himself because the usual custom was to send a junior officer who would put the new man up until he was posted. As it happened, C.B. drove me to the local hotel in a smart little dog cart and told me to come to dinner with him at 8-30 p.m. I made one of my many social gaffes that evening by arriving for dinner far too early and surprising my host on the verandah with a lady guest on his knee. However, no harm was done. I returned to the hotel in due course to sleep for the first time on a tape cot on a flat roof under a mosquito net. C.B. had told me that he had found a servant for me and sure enough in the morning the servant turned up. After inspecting my luggage, he told me that I had no clothes suitable for office or camp and he produced, Bezwire, a *durzi* who proceeded to measure me and produce patterns. We were interrupted by the entry of an exuberant Scot, George J. Campbell, who was the engineer in charge of surveys. After an exchange of greetings, he asked me what Bezwire was charging for the clothes but anticipating Campbell's indignation, Bezwire was flying for his life before I could answer. But Bezwire was a splendid man and worked for us for years until his death. Campbell said it was absurd to stop at the hotel and that I should move to the railway resthouse. In order to do so I must have equipment, so we departed to Mahomed Moosa, the principal store. I hinted that my financial resources were not over great but Campbell explained that my credit was good, so we bought bedding, cooking pots, table linen and crockery to be paid for later. I moved to the rest house next day. Like all railway resthouses it consisted of a big room in the centre, a bedroom with bathroom on each side and a deep verandah the whole length of the building. It had just the bare furniture needed; beds, chairs, tables, oil lamps and bathroom utensils. There was no electricity, water supply or sewerage in the India of those days. I remember being woken the first morning by my first buffalo rubbing himself against my cot. It was all very strange but wonderful."

The following day Lloyd Jones was to start on his work. It would be as well to explain something about the railway. Its full title was 'the Nizam's Guaranteed State Railway Co. Ltd.' In fact it was not a state railway but a British company with headquarters and a board of directors in London. The guarantee was commonplace where the share holders required some security from the state against the risk of development in unknown territory. It was not a large railway by Indian standards. Lines radiated from Hyderabad to join up with the Indian trunk routes. It was nevertheless a prosperous company paying its shareholders regular and good dividends.

The head of the railway in Secunderabad, called the Agent, was one, Pendlebury, a formidable character held in awe by all the staff. Under him was the Chief Engineer, already mentioned and then the district engineers and heads of various departments. Lloyd Jones was taken round the office to be introduced to the staff by the ever present George Campbell. The latter's younger brother, Gus, had also just joined the railway and it was decided that the two new arrivals should next fulfil that essential duty in all Indian stations, pay their calls. That the community was large, can be judged from the fact that it took three afternoons going round in a carriage leaving cards and where people were at home making their introductions and withdrawing as soon as politeness would allow. An exception was made at the residence of the Casson Walkers. He was Finance Member of the Nizam's Council of Ministers but he and his wife were out, leaving the honours to be done by their two lively daughters.They took advantage of the situation to invite the two young men to tea. It was not only Europeans who had to be called on. Lloyd Jones met two Indians, Abdulla Baig and Syed Hussain Bilgrami, who were to become life long friends.

Lloyd Jones was informed that he was posted to the Central Division of the railway under E.D. Puzey with headquarters in Secunderabad. In fact, he found he spent little time at headquarters – his work kept him busy out on line. When he was in Secunderabad he arranged to stay with another bachelor, E.M. Burn, Assistant Auditor, who had rented a house in cantonments. Lloyd Jones describes his experience of line work.

"I was anxious to get to work and was glad when Puzey returned from camp so that I was able to report for duty. Puzey was a bachelor who believed in taking things easily and not looking for trouble. He told me that I was to take over a sub-division from Secunderabad to Wadi, rather over a hundred miles but I gathered that he expected me to spend quite a lot of time in his office helping with his office work. Under pressure he agreed that I should attend to some work on the line which could not be started until it had been set out. So I left on the morning mail train, having arranged with the driver to set me down at the milage and pick me up in the evening on his way back. When the next day on my return I reported to Puzey, he was any thing but pleased and said he would take me out on some work at the week-end and show me how these expeditions should be arranged. Puzey's expedition was quite a different affair. We dined and slept in a saloon which was detached in the night at our destination station. After *chota hazri* (early breakfast) in the morning, we moved to the rest house and then by trolley to the work to be inspected, back to the

1. Cyril and Kathleen on the threshold of their Lalaguda bungalow shortly after taking up residence in 1908.

2. Cyril and Bill Walker working on the alignment of a new railway track.

3. Cyril in 1909.

4. Hyderabad city after the flood caused by the collapse of a dam, 1908.

5. Deaths following the flood, 1908.

6. Derrick engaged in bridge construction.

7. Secunderabad railways station.

8. His Exalted Highness the Nizam of Hyderabad.

9. Picnic at Hanging Rock. Cyril is on the left.

10. Christmas camp.

11. Cyril and Kathleen on a line inspection. Rosentbal is on the left with a stick.

12. Cyril, Kathleen and Michacl (centre, on the gun) with Mrs Wakefield (next to Kathleen) and Colin Wakefield at Daulatabad fort.

13. Visit of the London directors to see a new line (probably to Bidar) under construction.

14. Arrival at a rest home in 1910.

15. Salar Jung, Kathleen and Sir James Brungate at a garden party in 1933.

16. Cyril at his 100th birthday party in 1981.

rest house for tiffin (lunch) and then a book under a *punkah* until tea. A walk with guns over some scrub for partridge and quail finished the day."

The saloon referred to was a railway carriage divided into a large living compartment with easy chairs and dining table, separate sleeping compartment, bathroom, kitchen and servants quarter. They were attached to the regular trains to move from place to place. The trolley was a railway bogey with a bench fixed to it for the engineer to sit on. It was either pushed by collies or propelled by a system of levers.

"With this introduction I settled down to the routine work of my subdivision. My rank did not entitle me to the use of a saloon, so the drill was to go by train to a rest house and work from there, moving on from rest house to rest house as the work required. My two servants, four trolley men, trolley and cook box travelled with me. There was plenty of building and repair work to occupy my time but my over-riding responsibility was for the safety and running qualities of the track. I started with no knowledge whatever of permanent way or signalling. I fully realized my shortcomings and set about to remedy them. I had four permanent way inspectors, each in charge of about thirty miles of line and they willingly helped me. Like nearly all the men of that class, they were able and conscientious and I have always been grateful to them for helping me as they did. Year later, the daughter of one of them, Mary Weston, was my secretary and I saw her in England shortly before she died."

From the very start, although ready to learn the practical side of his work from those with experience, he was anxious to apply mathematical and engineering principles according to what he had learnt in college. Theoretical work he found of absorbing interest, occupying his leisure as well as his working hours. His colleagues content to rely on age old rule of thumb, watched this enthusiasm on the part of the youngster, no doubt, with cynical amusement. But they also knew of his superior qualifications and made no attempt to interfere.

Late in 1904, Richard Lloyd Jones died in the United States. This was a severe blow to the young man. His younger brother, Dick, went immediately over to America to do what had to be done after his father's death. Cyril wrote to his brother, "I suppose I have been called on to bear a sorrow as great as any I shall have to bear and I assure you it is as much as I can stand. All the same I am just behaving here as though nothing particular had happened. I hate sympathy from strangers and hate to show my sorrow. I think if our family were more demonstrative, we might feel less deeply." This bottling up of emotion is not so uncommon as he suggested. Even so, a young man of twenty-four, feeling home sick in a strange land, must have felt the loss of a parent very severely. Many years later, he used to take his son to a steak dinner at the Holborn Restaurant and explained with emotion that in just the same way his father had entertained him. Even allowing for the fact that the father had been for long periods away from home, the filial tie had been always strong.

Not less strong was the sense of family duty. Cyril was now head of the family and he was anxious to know whether his mother was properly provided for. He suggested that she might visit him in India during the cold weather. He worked out his budget carefully. His salary was Rs 350 per month (R1 = 1s - 3d approx.) and his travelling allowance Rs 150 per month. Since accommodation was provided and most of his servants, he reckoned that he could save as much as £ 250 a year. He was insistent that his youngest brother, Harold, should follow him to the Central and he was prepared to pay the fees as well as send something for his mother.

It should be remembered that at this time Lloyd Jones had no intention of staying permanently in India. He was still amassing experience. Shortly after his father's death he received a letter from America. It was from one of his cousins and he took it to be a letter of condolence. Trying to suppress the pain of his loss, he did not even read it and it got lost among his papers. Reading it some years later, he saw that it offered him a job in the U.S.A. and if he had read it at the time, he would have taken it up and left India for good. On what chance actions does the course of one's life depend! In fact, he had the opportunity to go to the States on several occasions but by that time he had become too attached to India.

Right from the beginning he was strongly attracted to the outdoor life out on the line. He has written about it, "I suppose my life was never so full of interest and so free of care as it was at this period." A description of the countryside gives some idea of its appeal. The Deccan, which is the geographical area including Hyderabad State, is a plateau stretching eastwards from the Western Ghats towards the Bay of Bengal and broken by a series of rivers, of which the Godavari and the Krishna are the most important, flowing south eastwards. With low hills and outcrops of volcanic rock it is scenically attractive. Apart from the river valleys, it is saved from the dense population of the Gangetic plain and with extensive areas of jungle provides excellent shooting. Moreover, the region is rich in historical remains, mainly stone fortresses built on hill tops, since it was the scene of continuous warfare in Moghul times.

For a young man naturally sociable and popular with his fellows it was a lonely life. After a hard day on the line with only subordinates for company, he spent his evenings in the bleak little rest houses, writing up his notes or trying to read by the flickering light of an oil lamp. Bombarded by insects and bats, he was driven early to his uncomfortable cot in an endeavour to sleep despite the melancholy howls of jackals and the occasional clatter of passing trains. Escape was provided by visits to Secunderabad for a day or two each month when he would enjoy the recreation and company supplied by the Club.

The lack of congenial companionship on line ceased with the posting of another young engineer on the adjoining section of line. Young Rosenthal happened to have interests similar to Lloyd Jones and they became firm friends. When opportunity arose they would have a get together for long discussions on philosophical subjects. Rosenthal, a Jew by race, was a Christian and religion was an absorbing topic. Lloyd Jones had retained his religious beliefs, though more of a speculative rather than a conformist nature. The sort of thing that roused their disputations was Strauss' *Life of Jesus* and works on Bible criticism. As happens with some young men, abstract theorising was more stimulating than the practical affairs of the world outside. In any case, they were largely cut off from current news and were quite happy to live in their own community of ideas. They were also required to learn Urdu but the only instructors available in the comparative wilds were village school masters. Although they did not become very proficient at the language, they gained a knowledge of how the country people lived.

Since the two men were on separate sections of line they could only meet on occasions and these were arranged as far as possible at some place of historical or scenic interest, or best of all where good shooting was available. They were beginners at the sport and restricted their quarry to game birds. With trepidation they once sat up for a panther and were rather relieved when the animal failed to keep the appointment. Lloyd Jones' guide of his early days decided to take them in hand and instruct them in *shikar*. Never one to follow his own teaching, George Campbell, having impressed on the young men the strict rule of limiting their field of fire when walking up partridge or snipe to the narrow sector immediately in front, on one occasion, shouting, "Duck, you blighters, duck!", shot right across them to bring down a bird on his opposite flank. In another connection, he had always advised courtesy and good manners towards the Indian staff. Yet when his train was unduly delayed at a station, he shouted vile abuse at the station master across a crowded platform. It was common experience in India that the trying climate could rouse violent temper at examples of crass stupidity or knavery in the mildest of men and George Campbell was not a mild man.

Given this quite satisfying life, Rosenthal could not understand Lloyd Jones' insistence on regarding his stay in India as a purely temporary matter and that soon he would be looking for a new job. The former's retort was "Good god, this is the softest job I've struck." However, despite an apparent divergence in temperament, the two men became life long friends. Uncle Rosie, as he was always affectionately known by the family, was to be the godfather of the second son, Michael.

Lloyd Jones was not left long to enjoy his experience of line work. As he explains, he was called into headquarters on special duty.

"It appeared that the Government of India had sanctioned a new scale of loading for the design of bridges and our Board had asked for a report on the strength of our girder bridges of spans from 20 ft. to 80 ft. in relation to the new loading. I suppose I was selected for this work in view of my experience of structural design. By this time, Dunlop had retired and I reported to Martin, who was acting until a new Chief was appointed. Martin was a good administrator and a good constructional engineer but his technical knowledge was negligible. All the plans were available so the calculations were made in a few hours and I found that the calculated stresses were in many cases far above the sanctioned limits. I consulted Martin and he agreed that I should take out the stresses for the loads actually using the bridges. This was a rather longer job because I had to collect diagrams of the rolling stock and estimate the effect on each span. I found on one section of 400 miles of line the stresses were in some respects far above the permitted limits. I drafted a report which Martin signed. Obviously the matter could not rest there but nothing much was done until the new Chief Engineer, Colonel Carew Smythe, was appointed and he saw that the report was sent home to the Board. It was quite obvious first, that the loads being carried by the bridges were greater than would be permitted by good practice, and second that the regulation method of calculating stresses in rivetted girders was unreliable. I concluded that the rivet stresses were reduced by sliding taking place over the rivetted surfaces and I applied the Calculus of Variations to calculate the effect of this assumption. It was this investigation which gained me the Watt Gold Medal from the Institute of Civil Engineers and brought me some credit from our consulting engineers who in the meantime had suggested an empirical rule for modifying the standard calculations. Before this, the Board had become alarmed and asked for a report after a thorough inspection of the girders had been made to detect any sign of overloading. This job also was handed to me and Smythe sent on my report under his signature to the Board. Precautionary measures were taken in the meantime in some cases and all the weak spans were removed within a year. It was this enquiry which started my interest also in the vibration of bridges in view of the unsatisfactory 'impact allowances' which were used in standard stress calculations."

Here at an early stage in his career by a piece of inventive calculation, recognized as such in the highest engineering circles, he marked himself out as quite exceptional. The intensity of his working life can better be illustrated by an extract from a letter to his mother at this time. "I had only a week in which to prepare the paper because, although the mathematical work was done, I had not even commenced to put the paper in a form for being read. At the same time, we were intensely busy at the office and, in consequence, I was working from six in the morning until the small hours of the night."

Curiously enough the letter suggests that what was occupying his attention more than this important work were his activities with the Volunteers. This was part time military training for European civilians, which was encouraged at the time, no doubt, with the Mutiny still in mind. Also it would provide congenial social recreation with much camping and drinking in the mess. Like every thing else he did, Lloyd Jones, joining as a subaltern, took his soldiering seriously. His initiation was comical. He appears to have acquired a lot of buttons and insignia for his uniform and he was in ignorance of the correct regulation wear. His servant was no wiser and seeking advice from other sahibs' servants, they took advantage of the situation by giving completely wrong instructions. The result was that the raw recruit appeared on parade with a motley arrangement of badges and accoutrement to the amusement of the rest of the parade.

Perhaps this spurred him on to showing his mettle and he proceeded to learn the drill book off by heart. He recorded that he was able to correct the drill sergeant in several respects while on parade which can hardly have endeared him to the regular officers in charge. One can detect this antipathy when the Adjutant reported adversely on him to the Colonel. However, when it came to the final tests before the Inspecting Officer, it was found impossible to fault him. This hostility towards him must have continued, because sometime later on being passed over for promotion, he resigned.

The desire to shine militarily seems to have seized people at the time. The Agent of the Railway, the redoubtable Pendlebury, became a Colonel. He was, in fact, an indifferent soldier but liked to be able to wear the uniform at official receptions and, moreover, it enhanced his wife's status in the community. Another factor was the hankering of some people to try out a career other than their own. A story is told of a district in British India where the District Magistrate became an officer in the Volunteers and enjoyed himself drilling the regular army units, while the Colonel in command of the military became an honorary magistrate and spent his time trying court cases.

Lloyd Jones returned to his former work on the line and the following is his account of the regular routine.

"An assistant engineer's work on open line was largely routine but there were usually some capital and major repair works on hand or under consideration. His day would start about 7 a.m. and he would be back by 6 p.m. and would then proceed to 'do the office box' which might take him an hour. A peon went daily between the engineer and the office carrying a box full of papers for the engineer's orders and signature. The work he had done during the day might have been inspecting the road and the work in progress, checking stores and labour, measuring work for payment or checking overseer's measurements. During the rains, there was the anxiety of flood damage to the line. Much of the country was irrigated from tanks (reservoirs) formed by closing a valley with an earth *bund* (dam). The tanks were anything from a few acres to a square mile in area and most of them had existed for centuries. There was always the danger that the failure of a *bund* or the blocking of a waste weir might cause the failure of other tanks lower down the valley and the sudden discharge of stored water to the railway crossing the valley. This possibility of flood damage needed constant vigilance and regular inspection of vulnerable places in the road. In my experience, the staff responded to the demand on them splendidly – the engineer, the permanent way inspector and the gangmen. A gang consisted of ten men under a *muccadam* (supervisor) in charge of three miles of line and their *izzat* (good name) depended on the safety and quality of their road. A *muccadam* would not hesitate to call out his men in the middle of the night, if he thought the road was in danger. Several times I have known the annual inspection train stopped at a gang so that the inspecting officer could compliment the gang on action they had taken in an emergency."

Routine was broken by certain incidents and special excursions.

"Puzey was an enthusiastic geologist, always expecting to discover a gold mine, and he persuaded me to use the Christmas holidays to go prospecting with him. We took the train to Guntakal, outside the

Hyderabad State, and went into camp. It was an unfortunate start because my servants left my camp bed in the train and I had to sleep on the ground for the rest of the trip. But it was a delightful tour. I was not very interested in the prospecting but we also visited the ancient ruined city of Humpi on the banks of the Tungabhadra river, which was full of interest. Years after, Puzey found his gold mine but it did not make him a rich man as it should have done. The Chief gave me another trip. He sent me to Trichur near Cochin in Malabar to inspect wooden sleepers and it was then that I had my only psychic experience – if indeed it was psychic. I had a two day train journey via Madras and reached Trichur on a short branch line. There was a man about my own age in the branch line carriage and I discovered that his name was Hewson, an assistant engineer on that line, the Madras Railway. He told me that there was no place to stay in Trichur but with him, so I thankfully accepted his invitation. The engineer in charge of the saw mill also lived in Trichur and he joined us for dinner. Over a game of bridge they told me what a queer place I had come to, the temperature was 80 degrees all the year round, the people polyandrists, absolutely truthful and practicing black magic. Hewson also told me that the bungalow was haunted but he would not tell me what form the haunting took. It seemed significant, however, that my servant sought permission to sleep at the railway station. Hewson woke me in the morning and drew my attention to a bridge table at the side of my bed, the cloth of which had been slashed with a knife while I slept. He said that whenever he occupied the bungalow something was destroyed by cutting. In this case, as I slept on the verandah, the act could be easily accomplished. The next night I sat up reading in bed and only went to sleep as the sun rose. When I woke an upholstered chair by my bed had been slashed. I had placed it there with a gun resting on the arms. The third night, in spite of the heat, we both slept inside the bungalow and secured all the doors and windows. In the morning, although we could find no sign of entry, Hewson's dressing gown near his bed was slashed in strips."

"He learnt later that Hewson refused to go on occupying the bungalow which was pulled down. Haunted rest houses in India were no rarity. Lloyd Jones' story had a sequel. When he was travelling back to England on leave, he met an English nurse on board ship. She had been looking after an Indian lady and another woman in the *zenana* (women's quarters) had had a spell cast on her. The effect of this was that she kept finding articles of clothing and other fabrics cut into strips. In some cases, the damaged articles had been in locked trunks, the locks remaining intact.

The police were called in but Sherlock Holmes not being among their number the case remained unsolved."

"On my way back from Trichur I visited Conoor in the Nilgiri Hills to call on Gales who was constructing the rack railway up from Metapolium and went on to Silks Hotel in Ooty. I was not very thrilled with the construction but I was charmed with Ooty and the countryside. Although it was the cold season – November 1906 – it had been quite hot in the plains and the change to Ooty at 8000 ft. was wonderful. Wandering along the deserted roads and lanes, I could imagine myself back in England and then I would return to a wood fire in my sitting room.

Christmas was near, when the offices were closed for a week and it was our custom to spend our time in camp shooting. This year we decided to have a camp in the jungle at Rasnum near Dharur. I had now met Bill Walker, who had been appointed a few months before me and had been away on a survey and he decided to join us. A new engineer was due out in Christmas week, named Mitchel, so I arranged to meet him and take him out to camp with us. All went well and as usual we thoroughly enjoyed ourselves. We all became life long friends. Earlier in the year, Bill Walker had saved me from what would probably have been death by drowning. A storm had swamped the skiff in which I had been rowing on the Hussain Sagar Lake. I had not tried to swim since school days and I soon became entangled in the weeds. Walker swam out with a rope and I was pulled on to the bank. He came from Tasmania and had been educated in Edinburgh. He was a fine man and a good engineer.

We visited many other beautiful and interesting places in the three years before I went on leave in 1907 but that did not absorb all our time off duty. I had bought Martin's pony and trap and spent most morning exercising the pony when I was in Secunderabad. Rosenthal's District Engineer, Shaffer, had imported a Locomobile, an American steam car, and this gave us some amusement. It must have been the first car in Hyderabad State and Shaffer brought it by train to his headquarters at Kazipet. There was only one road about ten miles long and Shaffer's practice was to send out men to station themselves at intervals along the road to assist in case of breakdown. I don't think they were ever needed, but of course, you can never tell with a strange piece of machinery. I remember one occasion when an Indian friend induced Shaffer to bring his car to take part in a wedding procession at Warangal, the destination of the road. It was a great success, though I had to work the feed pump by hand from the back seat."

On the subject of early motoring, Lloyd Jones told a story of how in one small station the only two cars met at the only cross road and had a collision. Also when he himself was out motoring in the remote countryside his car broke down. The only person to repair it was the village blacksmith, who, although he had never seen such a contraption before, managed to do what was necessary. It might be wise to enter a caveat when relating his stories by repeating what a close friend said many years later, "I know you despise truth as a superfluous ingredient in the pleasure afforded by a good story."

"The young engineers of my rank were not really interested in the social life of Secunderabad; there was too much to interest them elsewhere. There were very few unmarried girls in the station and I mostly dined and associated with men of my own age, occasionally at a regimental mess. I was on the guard of honour of the Prince of Wales when he visited Hyderabad in February 1906 and attended the review and levée. I think, however, I was much more impressed by a visit which took place the following week. It was when I had occasion to investigate the site for a new station at Sirnapalli, within the estate of a *Rani* and Campbell said that he knew the Rani and would like to join me. We sent her a message to say we were coming and when we were within a few miles of her place we were met by her servants. It was about midday and they had cleared a space in the jungle and laid out a meal. I think I never enjoyed a meal more. About three or four Indian dishes on leaf plates were followed by the most delicious sweetmeats. We then mounted ponies which the Rani had sent for us and rode to the palace where the Rani received us in durbar. She was a charming middle aged woman but unfortunately was a victim of elephantiasis. I bitterly regretted that I had to rely on Campbell to express my appreciation but he was fluent in Urdu and I was not. She and Campbell got on very well and were obviously renewing an old friendship. Her kindness and hospitality was only typical of my experience of all Indians I met in the next thirty years."

The account of the Prince of Wales' visit is dealt with more fully in a letter to his mother dated February 15, 1906, "On Friday I got up quite early and attended the Review in uniform. The Review was quite exciting. There were about 9000 troops out altogether; three British infantry, one British cavalry regiment, two batteries Field Artillery, one battery Horse Artillery and the remainder were native infantry and cavalry. The Prince and the Nizam were there with a very fine escort and native attendant officers. All went very well except the gallop past. The general gave a furious gallop instead of the regulation 12 miles per hour. The horse artillery went by at full gallop in splendid form but the cavalry was a mere horde of horsemen. Each regiment which should have been in two long lines, consisted of two ragged lines and a rabble of horsemen in the middle. Men who know, say it was quite disgraceful. It looked very fine, of course, because the pace was so great. While the 2nd Imperial Service Cavalry (native) passed by, one man's horse fell, bringing down a second. The first man was hurt and eventually died the same day. The conduct of the second man was quite good; he stood over his comrade in the face of two regiments of charging cavalry and in consequence the cavalry passed round them without damage. The Prince, I believe, was most fearfully sick over the accident. Walker succeeded in obtaining an invitation to the reception in the evening and we went together. There were about two hundred people there. We were all presented to the Prince and Princess in turn and they both shook hands most graciously. We then witnessed a GCSI bestowed by the Prince on Casson Walker, the Finance Minister. The Prince and Princess stayed about a half hour longer and then departed. It seemed quite curious for the Prince and Princess to be chatting in a drawing room like ordinary folk. They both seemed very agreeable, the Princess particularly looked really nice and every inch a Princess. She seemed to be literally covered in diamonds. I certainly would not have missed the show for a good deal.

I am sending you a time table in order to give you an idea of the precautions taken. The whole line is lined with sentries of the military police who stand with fixed bayonets at the present as the train passes whether at night or day. These sentries are within sight of each other – a quarter mile apart – and are there day and night for two days before. Besides this the railway gangs patrol the line, one man every quarter of a mile and the Inspectors have to trolley over shortly before the train is due. Luckily we got the Prince over without any accident."

Clearly the young man was more impressed by Royalty than his subsequent account would suggest. Alternatively he may have thought that his mother, living in a London suburb, would be interested by such, an account.

"To continue with the narrative – "nearly every weekend, I went on some expedition. Bill Walker and I bicycled to Nizamabad one day, about a hundred miles over a dirt road, sending our kit and servants by train. Bicycles were not much used in the districts at that time and we created some astonishment. We also discovered that tea brewed in aluminium flasks acts as a violent emetic. On another weekend, we joined Rosenthal on a visit to the hill fort at Kondapalli near Bezwada. We had often visited this fort before, which had been occupied by Clive and had relics of his stay, but this time instead of climbing the face of the hill, we took a long disused track up through the jungle, a beautiful route and marvellous view from the top. There is a photo of us sitting there. We slept in the fort and in the evening watched a panther on the other side of the ravine. As a result, Rosenthal woke in the night and thinking that I was not in my cot, called to Walker in the cot beside him, 'Jonah's been lifted by the panther.' Walker waking with difficulty muttered, 'Oh bother Jonah' and went to sleep again. I was awake and my chuckles reassured Rosenthal."

Lloyd Jones was brought in from line work to Secunderabad head office.

"My duties when Personal Assistant to the Chief Engineer were mainly to prepare cases for the C.E.'s orders and to see that effect was given to his orders. I had one executive responsibility in connection with the Engineering Workshops (E.W.S.). The E.W.S. had grown from small beginnings to quite a considerable size but continued to be a kind of side show of the C.E.'s office. I found that it was being run quite honestly but very inefficiently. The work was done on work orders not only of the various officers of the Engineering Department but by any officer who found it convenient and the cost of the work done was charged to the indenting officer. The result was that there was no proper review of the costs. I put up a report and as a result, Frank Buckley was appointed Workshop Superintendent. He was a young married man who had been a foreman in the Daimler works and he was a great success. I also found time to carry out tests on rivetted girders. The paper I had sent to the Institute of Civil Engineers had contained the suggestion, that under high stress, slipping took place over the rivetted surfaces and if this was so, it would change the form of the curve in which the girder deflected under load. My experiments were to detect the change and to measure the amount of slip. They were quite successful but I found no opportunity to publish the results. By that time, my interest had moved to the permanent way problem and I had begun some experiments on fishplates. Many different designs of fishplates were in use on our railway and on other Indian railways and I could find no one who could explain the merits of the different patterns, so I decided to test how they behaved under load. The method was to compare the deflections under load of a length of rail with an equal length of the same rail with a fishplate joint in the middle. The two specimens were forced apart with a screw jack and the deflections of both rails measured. I used the same instrument to measure the deflections as I had used for the girder tests; it was a simple mirror deflectometer which I had made in the bazaar for a few rupees. The fishplate tests were most interesting and I continued them for several years. I sent the results to the Institute of Civil Engineers and was awarded the Indian Premium for the paper. During this period I commenced writing a kind of manual for the department which I issued from time to time as circulars under the Chief Engineer's signature. One I issued some years later on estimating depreciation was reprinted (without acknowledgement) as an appendix to the Government of India Public Works Code."

This account illustrates two characteristics. He was never content to accept existing practices without fully testing them and submitting them to scientific analysis. His enquiring mind continually sought improvements or at least a logical and mathematically proved justification for the established state of affairs. It was never sufficient in his opinion that because something had gone on from time immemorial, it should be allowed to continue. The other characteristic which became more marked as he rose in the railway, was his business sense. He was always sensitive to costs and every expenditure had to be shown to be justified before it was sanctioned.

The general condition of life in Secunderabad and some of the hazards are described.

"These years had not been free from trouble. We had a bad cholera epidemic one year and once was enough. I had expected that one would be either alive and well, or else dead, but it was not like that. While the epidemic lasted the whole station seemed to be suffering from intestinal disorders and you expected it at any time to develop into cholera. One came to the Club each evening apprehensive to know who was missing. In those days, there was no preventive and no real treatment. The epidemic did not last long but it was a most unpleasant experience. Plague and malaria did not trouble Hyderabad until after 1907 but we were warned to protect ourselves from typhoid. All water and milk were boiled and we did not use cream or butter uncooked. In general, we did not eat any food that was not hot from the stove; no cold meat, salads or sweetmeats, but plenty of fruit. Two railway officers contracted typhoid but they recovered. We lost one Assistant Engineer who died of meningitis within a month of arrival and another whose trolley was run down by a light engine.

During the last three years I had been living very amicably with Eric Burn, who had moved to a bungalow in the railway suburb of Lalaguda. My bare living expenses were about Rs 150 per month, say Rs 50 for food, Rs 50 for servants and Rs 50 for rent and sundries. This was hardly more than I drew for travelling allow (Rs 5 per day). However I was not able to save my pay which had risen to Rs 500 per month because I had to buy equipment and pay for my amusements: cartridges, pony, club, entertainments etc. and 12½% of my salary went as subscription to the Provident Fund. Single men could live well on an Assistant Engineer's pay. Burn ran the chummery well and the servants looked after me when I was touring. I had two difficulties to begin with. One servant absconded while I was travelling and I never discovered the reason. Another I suspected of robbing me and the police ran him in but the Indian magistrate discharged him. He said either I should learn to speak better Urdu or hire a servant who spoke better English. He was probably right and the trouble arose from a misunderstanding. These two incidents must have been due to my inexperience because in nearly forty years in every way my servants served me faithfully and well."

Married Life

By 1907 Lloyd Jones was due for three months home leave and since he had earned promotion to District Engineer on a salary of Rs. 700 to Rs. 900 per month (£560 to £700 per year), he felt that he was in a position to get married. Nothing much has been said about the young man's relations with Kathleen Penty during the three years he was in India. He wrote to her regularly but unfortunately these letters have not survived. He sent her presents, though in a letter to his mother he wrote that he had been unable to find a decent ring for her and anyway he did not much believe in that sort of thing. It did not seem to occur to him that his fiancée might think otherwise. All along he was quite convinced that Kathleen would be ready, if not eager, to join him in India. Because he so enjoyed life on the line with its sense of adventure and open air activity, he seemed to take it for granted that she would. The real reason for his confidence, of course, was that the young couple were in love. That she had waited seven years for him was surely sufficient test of her devotion. In fact, Kathleen, a pretty girl, had made many friends and had another suitor, a poet, no less. That the conflicting claims must have been serious at one time is suggested by Cyril writing that if she had any doubts she was at liberty to break off their engagement. Hardly the attitude of an ardent lover, one might think, but, in fact, a mark of high principle since the young man was genuinely in love and Kathleen always said that it was his determination and strong will that won her over.

Before going on leave, Lloyd Jones was sufficiently sure of the position, to write to his future father-in-law to ask for his permission to marry his daughter and then to her, instructing her to fix a date. The account of the leave and wedding is brief.

"I arrived at Victoria on 24th March 1907, and was met by five faithful men friends who had seen me off three years before and my two brothers. I collected Kathleen from her flat and took her to my mother's house at Wood Green. I spent the next month visiting friends and relations and entertaining Kathleen and her sisters. The Chairman was friendly and the Consulting Engineers (Rendle and Robertson) particularly cordial. I lunched with John Hall in Manchester, for whose firm I had prepared a section book, and he offered me a job. It was to take charge of a concern he was starting which became the British Reinforced Concrete Company but I was not tempted to leave India. I went to York on 7th May and was married the next day. We spent a week in Harrogate and left Victoria for Marseilles and the *S.S. China* on 23rd May. Ralph Freeman was the only friend to see me off but some of Kathleen's admirers were there. The voyage was very pleasant in spite of the heat. One of the passengers was Queenie Jeffries who was going to Hyderabad to take charge of a girl's school, which the Nizam's Government was starting for girls in purdah. She became our very great friend. We arrived in Bombay on 7th June. George Campbell gave us dinner at Victoria Terminus and we left the same night for Hyderabad. At Secunderabad, we stayed with the Agent and two days later left for my headquarters at Kazipet in a saloon which was allotted to me as District Engineer.

The advent of Kathleen extended my view of India. Hitherto it had meant to me the romance and sport of the jungle, my work with its technical problems and the society of my men friends. From now on it would be different. The Agent had a dinner party for us when we arrived and as soon as we reached my district, we were bidden to a party by the Manager of the Singareni colliery near by. In a short time, I found that Kathleen had made a group of friends, people previously little known to me. The explanation was that in Hyderabad society young men were common while young women were scarce. I found that even my association with my old colleagues seemed to take on the air of a social function. I did not resent the change, I rather liked it so long as it did not interfere with my work. So far as possible, I took Kathleen with me on my work, frequently taking long journeys by trolley and she took to it very well.

She had her first practical experience of what an engineer's work was like when we dined with Davies, the Colliery Manager, at Yellendu about 60 miles from Kazipet. It was 15th June, five weeks after our wedding and the monsoon had just broken. As we started our dinner, a telegram was handed to me saying that the line had been breached at mile 160 and that a goods train to Madras had been derailed. We finished dinner, went to bed in the saloon and had it taken to mile 160, about 120 miles away. It was a bad derailment but no one had been hurt and my work did not start until the Loco Department had cleared the track which it was thought would take 24 yours. I spent the day with the P.W.I. arranging for men and materials for an early start at day break next day. My saloon was still at the site of the derailment and we had dinner and went to bed. I was woken by the Indian driver of the derailed engine knocking at my window. He explained that the site had been cleared and that work on the track could begin but that my men would not start without orders from the P.W.I. who had gone home to bed. I told him that we had arranged to start in the morning and that any way it was not his concern. He said that if I came out and gave the necessary orders and sat under a tree, we could pass the Madras Mail in the morning on time. I surrendered and the morning Mail was passed through on time with the absent P.W.I. on the foot plate. George, the Loco Superintendent, to whom I reported the incident in full, was devoted to his men and saw to that driver's future. I remembered the advice I had been given on my way out to India on the *S.S. Peninsular*, and I hope I never gave occasion again to be reminded of my duty. It was raining all this time and I now took Kathleen home from her dinner party."

This account of Kathleen's early days in India is over complacent. Imagine an young and lively girl accustomed to a sophisticated existence in London being suddenly transported to a remote outpost in India. The country was strange and in many respects frightening. She was not able to get used to it gradually in a comparatively civilized station like Secunderabad. In Kazipet, which was a junction on the Nizam's Railway, she had no White company except for her husband, who was working all day and probably in the evenings as well. The nearest company, and that too male, was at the coal mines some sixty miles away. They had to live in an antique rest house with a thatched roof harbouring all kinds of vermin and snakes. Servants would do the housework and shopping, and so she was left to amuse herself from her own resources. Her husband exaggerated the charms of life on line – trundling slowly along on a trolley through the heat of the day or tramping through the jungle with a gun – hardly a glamorous alternative to consorting with interesting and amusing people of her own age, interspersed with theatres, concerts and art exhibitions. In fact, Kathleen was miserably unhappy and seriously thought of leaving her husband and returning to England. Little wonder, therefore, that, as suggested later, she petitioned to be moved to Secunderabad.

To continue with Lloyd Jones' account, "The accident at mile 160 was the first time I had to deal with an accident caused by flood damage, and obviously we had to see that this kind of accident did not occur again. Eventually an excellent patrol system was adopted to be brought into use during the rains and at any other time that danger threatened. It was worked out by Rosenthal and during the next forty years no train was derailed by flood damage. Although frequently, flood damage occurred but trains were stopped in time. Unfortunately fifty years later, when we had all left India, a disastrous accident occurred quite near mile 160 in which over a hundred passengers were drowned but I was reliably informed that the patrol system which Rosethal had introduced was not then in use. Another lesson from the 1907 accident, was the need for a history of every flood opening to be readily available and I provided for this in the manual I issued from the Chief Engineer's Office sometime later.

During the next six months, Kathleen accompanied me on most of my inspections and we managed to include a fair amount of sight seeing. We frequently had some girl friend accompanying us. At the end of August, we had a most successful trip to the Kondapalli fort, already mentioned. The party included Queenie Jeffries, Walker and Rosenthal. The village at the foot of the hill was renowned for its *nautch* (dancing girls), famous all over India, and some of them entertained us after dinner in the ruined fort where we were spending the night. In Christmas week, we had a big party at Kazipet, comprising a dozen, including Queenie and two of her teachers. We managed to get to Secunderabad about twice a month. We went to several dances, a military parade, dined at the Residency, attended a reception and garden party for the Viceroy and a Hyderabad Volunteer Regiment at home and dinner. We saw quite a lot of Queenie and of Mrs Sarojini Naidu, who was a close friend of Queenie–she was just a poet then and had not taken up politics. Kathleen stayed with Queenie one week when I was in Madras. I had gone there to attend a meeting of the Board of Studies as I was examining in several subjects for the Madras Engineering College. I did this for several years but I was not a success. I was not really interested and I did not have the time to do the work properly. About a week before Christmas, my colleagues gave me a dinner to celebrate the award of the Watt Gold Medal and the Chief presided.

I was astonished early in the new year (1908) to be transferred back to Secunderabad as Personal Assistant to the Chief Engineer, the job I had held as an Assistant Engineer, although I was now confirmed as a District Engineer. I thought that perhaps it was because the Chief Engineer could not get on without me but later I had reason to think it was because Kathleen was tired of Kazipet and had brought her influence to bear on the C.E.. I was sorry because it meant leaving unfinished work in which I was particularly interested. However, it was convenient because Richard was about to be born in April and we went to live with Dr Hunt, the railway doctor, whose wife was in England.

By this time, the company had recruited six or eight more engineers, young unmarried men, and the advent of Kathleen seemed to give them ideas. Several wrote to their girl friends, telling them to get a few things together and to come to Hyderabad to get married. One of them had misgivings when the proposal was accepted. He wired to his fiancée to leave the boat at Aden, as he had changed his mind, and to go back home again. He got a reply that she had not changed hers and he was to meet her in Bombay. He did so and they were happy ever after. Nearly all our engineers were married within a year or so. Bill Walker and Rosenthal remained single, as they had no girl friends at home and could not fix up any thing locally. In the meantime, my son, Richard, was born and I built a bungalow for us on the side of the hill at Lalaguda. As Richard was born in April, Kathleen spent that hot weather in the plains but it was the only time she did so."

Something should be said about the European community centred on Secunderabad. The railway staff are mostly mentioned individually. They married and had families and it was undoubtedly an extremely congenial and pleasant society. They were joined by some non-railway residents, such as Frank Crawford of the police, Durand of the College and Macpherson of the Bank, who all became close friends. An unusual feature for an Indian station was that people remained there for their whole careers, whereas in most places frequent transfers prevented long lasting friendships. From photographs of picnics, shooting parties and other outdoor functions, it is apparent that they were a good looking crowd despite the outlandish clothes of the period. Yet amorous intrigues, common enough in such communities in India, are not recorded as having upset the social harmony–certainly no divorces occurred. The strength of friendships can best be testified to by their lasting long after

India with frequent visits and regular correspondence during retirement to the U.K. and other parts of the world.

Secunderabad had a large European community – the Club membership was about 300, although this would include a few Indians. The military would provide a large proportion, mixing not so closely with the civilians and, in any case, they were a moving population. Recreation consisted, as one would expect in India, of outdoor sport and games. Riding was not so popular with the railway people, though most would keep ponies and traps before the advent of motor cars. With the military, however, polo was the great game. Target shooting was popular, at which Kathleen shone, burdening her side board with a fine array of silver trophies. Tennis, golf and swimming were the other main activities. Evening entertainment was more restricted. Dinner parties were favoured rather than mere drinks and afterwards those present would perform their party pieces, which mostly consisted of baritone and soprano solos. Lloyd Jones for a time attempted the mandolin. Over the years, the same faces combined with the same repertoires must have become wearing, however friendly the parties. Amateur theatricals were popular and from time to time touring companies would perform to eager audiences starved of cultural nourishment.

Lloyd Jones with his intellectual turn of mind complained of lack of interests, although, in fact, he found little time for reading, being too occupied with his engineering research. He noted that conversation was confined to purely local subjects and among men mostly to 'shop'. Concern with outside affairs in the world at large was minimal. English newspapers took three weeks to arrive by which time reports had lost their topicality. A return to the centre of activity and the source of entertainment and cultural interests was the main inducement to take home leave as soon as was possible.

Now follows an interesting account of the Hyderabad floods – "The monsoon of 1908 was disastrous not only for railway but for Hyderabad City. The city proper is on the south bank of the river Moosey but it has extended for a mile north of the river. Exceptional rain fell for several days. Flood water came down the river and during the night, overflowed the north bank into that part of the city which as the water rose was largely destroyed drowning many of the inhabitants. The death was in thousands and for days, bodies were recovered from the ruins, from up tress and for miles along the banks of the river, where villagers were retrieving them for the sake of ornaments found on the bodies. At the time of the disaster, I knew nothing of this. I was holding the fort for the Chief who was in

Madras. Telegrams were coming in of damage to the line. The Kazipet Division was worst hit and the District Engineer in charge was isolated by breaches. I started out with an engine and saloon to give what help I could from the Secunderabad side. We passed over one river in flood and as the water was rising at the next station we came to, we steamed out again onto higher ground where the train halted for the night. In the morning we got to Bibinagar River which was spanned by a bridge of ten 20 foot girders. It was a curious sight with a mass of uprooted palm trees brought down by the flood forming a dam across the bridge piers. The rising water had breached the railway bank behind the abutment. Naturally it was a large breach because it had taken the whole of the river discharge. I could not take the relief train any further but we managed to get a trolley over the breach and went on to see what more damage there was. I found ten or more bridges and culverts gone in the next fifty miles. I was then thirty miles from the District Engineer at Kazipet and I wired him that I would deal with the damage that I had already come across.

It was several weeks before the line was restored for traffic and in the meantime the Chief had returned and was staying on the east side of Kazipet where there was also heavy damage. I arranged with the P.W.I.s to collect all the labour they could get from the villages and then I returned to Secunderabad to mobilize staff and collect tools and sand bags. At one bridge, four 20 foot girders had been washed off their piers and had to be recovered from the jungle and re-erected. I sent out a foreman and men from the workshops to do this job. The offices also supplied men who could act as pay clerks and store clerks. But the bulk of the work would have to be done with *powrah* (mattock) and basket and I wanted more supervisors, so I telegraphed the other D.E.s, who were repairing their damage, to send any help they could. In response, Sewell from Jalna Division came down to Bibinagar with one of his P.W.I.s. He was a little critical of the start we had made but I was relieved to leave him to fill up the hole which he did most expeditiously. Our west end was completed before the rest of the line was ready and the office staff boasted that every rupee and item of stores had been properly accounted for. This incident was important to me apart from the adventure and experience. When the Chief came through, he took what I had done as a matter of course, neither complimentary nor critical, which was what I had expected of him. But afterwards in his report to the Board, he mentioned every other officer who had been engaged, except me. I did not see the report until long after it had been issued, which itself was unusual, and even then I hardly noticed the omission. Later I realized its significance. I knew that I had risen to the emergency perfectly well and that nothing I had done had been criticized. If the Chief did not think well of me in these circumstances, he never would and that I could not depend on him for promotion."

The events leading up to going on leave in June 1911 are recounted. "My marriage not only to some extent changed the pattern of my life,it also changed my outlook. Before, I had not worried over much about my pay and prospects. I merely wanted interesting work and play. I now felt that I had a stake in the world and responsibilities that went with it. I continued my engineering researches and spent much of my spare time in a shed at the railway workshops, getting real satisfaction from some of the results. But I also enjoyed my social life. We were seldom alone in our bungalow. Bill Walker lived with us for a time and his widowed sister from Sidney spent some months with us. Nell Haughton was another visitor we liked very much.

In 1910, I took over an open line division with headquarters at Secunderabad to carry out the renewal of some 80 miles of track. I was friendly with 61st Pioneers who were stationed at Secunderabad at that time and Lt. Colonel Brooking who was commanding suggested that we should use his men. The Chief agreed and Brooking lent us Lieutenant Storey, one of his officers, to look after the men. It was a great success and the renewal was completed in record time and at low cost.

There was nearly a tragedy at that time. We were spending Christmas in a shooting camp with a few friends at Dornakal, when Dr Hunt telegraphed advising me that Kathleen and Richard should go at once to Conoor for anti-rabic treatment, as our small terrier, which we had sent to him for examination, had died of rabies. Luckily Nell Haughton, who was one of our party, was able to accompany them and they left immediately on their forty eight hour journey to the Hills. When the party returned some weeks later, I met them at Wadi and found them very hungry, having spent the last of their cash the previous evening on creme de menthe, instead of buying themselves dinner.

I had a year's furlough due to me in the spring of 1911 and we had decided to take it in England as soon as it was due. I normally would not have taken long leave but I was worried about my prospects. I liked my Chief, Carew Smythe, very much and I certainly served him well but I was convinced that I could not look to him for any thing special in the way of promotion. What convinced me was that in 1910, Puzey was due back from leave and was to act as Chief for Smythe who was going on leave. The ship, *Trieste,* on which Puzey was coming back, was overdue in the

Indian Ocean and believed lost. To meet the loss of Puzey, revised postings were issued and I found that I was not included. The *Trieste* turned up a week or so later, towed into Bombay with a missing propeller, so the revised postings were cancelled. To me the inference was clear. I had now the responsibilities of a family and I must find a job with better prospects. My information was that Canada offered work and I had met two Canadians who would give me letters to Canadian railway people, so I decided to try there."

Long leave and the War years

"I sailed to Canada in July, just after the coronation of George V. I enjoyed the voyage and people I met and was particularly charmed with the passage up the St Lawrence to Montreal. During the voyage I began to ponder an event which had occurred just before I sailed and which I had disregarded at the time. In compliance with rules I had applied to my Board for permission to obtain employment during my leave. On giving permission, the office told me that the Chairman wanted to see me before I left. I told the Chairman that I intended to get work in Canada to widen my experience. After wishing me success and some general talk, the Chairman said that the Board hoped I would not stay in Canada and that I had excellent chances of promotion in India as the Agent was an old man and would not be remaining much longer. Very stupidly I had not been impressed by these remarks at the time but thinking them over I realized their significance. The Chairman would not have troubled himself merely to be friendly. The explanation could only be that the Board seriously considered appointing me to succeed Carew Symthe, who would succeed Pendlebury, the Agent. I was just 30 so that this indeed was a splendid chance which changed my ideas of employment in Canada, although I still intended to get temporary work for the experience. I had no difficulty in obtaining an appointment as Assistant Engineer with the Canadian Northern Railway. As I had not to report for a week or two, I visited my relatives in Scranton, Pennsylvania, and was made most welcome. I discussed my prospects with my cousin, Edward Jones, and largely on his advice decided against the Canadian Northern appointment in favour of another course I had in mind. Consequently after spending some very pleasant weeks visiting my relatives, I returned to England.

The alternative course, which I now took, was to continue my education. I could not find the facilities I really wanted for post-graduate work but I was able to join the London School of Economics (L.S.E.) for courses in economics, statistics, economic history and political ideas, the last of which under Dickinson. At University College (U.C.), I took mathematical physics under A.N. Whitehead. The latter, whose brother was the Bishop of Madras, was very kind to me and entertained us at his flat. I attended a course of lectures on aerodynamics at U.C. and at the conclusion, the lecturer offered me a job at Vickers and found difficulty in understanding my preference for work on an Indian railway.

So Kathleen and I settled down to spending our long leave as students. Kathleen at the Slade School and I at the L.S.E. and the U.C. We managed to borrow accommodation from friends. Bill Walker's brother lent us his small house in South London and after that Gertie Boart, an old friend of Kathleen, lent us her flat off the Fulham Road. We spent most evenings at the theatre in the pit, costing half a crown. We spent the summer, I think, at Filey and altogether we had a most enjoyable time until we had to return to India in June 1912."

Lloyd Jones in after life laid great stress on the value of the year's sabbatical. It broadened his knowledge and extended his interests into fields which he found of great value as his career developed beyond pure engineering into general management, where he had to deal with men engaged in politics and higher administration. It also opened his eyes to opportunities available should he choose, but India had already fastened too strong a grip on him and he could not be tempted to go elsewhere.

"Early in 1913, the Agent, Pendlebury, died and as I anticipated, Smythe was appointed Agent and Chief Engineer. I was made head of the Engineering Department with the rank, pay and responsibilities of Chief but without the designation. I never discovered the reason for this but the Board did the same thing when I succeeded Smythe. The change came easily as I had worked with Smythe for so long already."

Promotion meant the removal of financial worries, especially with regard to the cost of educating the children in England. The second son was born in 1914. The salary of acting Chief Engineer was Rs 1200 per month. They were living in the same house in Lalaguda but were able to have it extended and improved, including the installation of a fire place, although, in fact, it was never cold enough to need a fire. Kathleen's artistic skills came into play with the decorations such as hand stensilled curtains. Finally with great pride the latest in motor cars, a model T Ford, was acquired.

"A very sad event occurred early in 1914. Our friend and neighbour, Violet Burn, died of rabies. This made us all specially cautious of strange dogs and explains why our servant roused us early one morning to say that there was a dog on the verandah and he thought it was rabid. I said I would look into it later, when Kathleen surprised me by calling out `Fetch me the gun, boy' and striding out in her night clothes, shot the animal dead.

When war broke out the effect was immediate. There were no dances or big parties for the next four years. People were continually moving and there was a general air of gloom and anxiety. We probably were less affected than most people because we had so many interests unaffected by war. Even our diet was little affected. Anxiety for relatives and friends was, of course, general. Richard's education became a problem but we were able to engage an excellent teacher who remained with us until the end of the war.

I had taken over full powers and responsibilities of Chief Engineer and I think as an engineer this six years was probably my most interesting period. Although new construction and surveys had been stopped as far as possible, there was plenty to occupy us. The monsoon of 1914 brought abnormal floods in the Godavari valley and the girders were washed off the piers of the Purna bridge, stopping through traffic on the metre gauge (narrow gauge) line to Manmad. Luckily we had some old Warren girders, which had been removed from the broad gauge line many years before. These were repaired, converted to metre gauge and erected on the piers of the Purna bridge. The original girders were retrieved from the river, repaired and replaced on the bridge. I used rather unusual methods, calling for special skill from the executive staff and led by Davis, the engineer in charge, they all responded magnificently. Some of the photographs thrill me still. One of the operations demanded meticulous accuracy from 44 groups of men specially trained to carry out certain tasks simultaneously – tasks of which they had no previous experience. They reacted successfully and with enthusiasm. This was not the end of the matter as the bridge had to be made safe for the future, an exercise full of interest both theoretical and practical.

Another somewhat similar operation came up towards the end of my time as Chief Engineer. It was to place the 34 spans of 80 ft girders on the piers of the Krishna bridge which had recently been completed. The method I used was also rather unusual. A suitable derrick car was constructed from material available in our stores and scrap yards. It travelled on the railway track and placed each fully completed span of 50 tons on its piers. The work was completed at a fraction of the time and cost of any alternative method and the derrick was used for every regirdering job we had for years after. There is a photo of the car in front of one of the Government of India annual administrative reports. I drew the design myself and it was the last drawing I made and the first after a lapse of twenty years."

Lloyd Jones catalogues other engineering work for which he was responsible. "Construction work at Secunderabad involved a large marshalling yard. The war prevented the import of steel for bridging and designs had to be prepared for constructing the viaducts out of girders previously removed from the line during bridge renewals. In view of my previous experience, I took particular interest in the drawing office and was able to make several suggestions for expediting work. One which pleased my staff was a graphical method of designing small water supply networks, which was a frequent task. I must have worried the general office too, because I reorganized the record system and reconstructed the office buildings. I may explain that many years before the railway had taken over the buildings of the old military cantonment and used them as offices. We greatly improved ours by removing the interior walls. Without any suggestion from us the other railway offices were soon adopting our record system and clamouring for their buildings to be altered.

I found time to continue the study of the more general technical questions which affected us, such as steel sleeper failures, bridge stresses and discharge from catchments. The study of catchments included the use of our extensive records, supplemented by field surveys, flood measurements and rainfall intensity measurements. This research was for our own special problems but sometimes conclusions of general interest emerged, although we had no time to put them in a form for publication. Sometimes these special investigations led to unexpected results. On one occasion, what we thought was a highly technical enquiry into the high cost of gas making disclosed a hole in the underground gas main. On another occasion, an elaborate enquiry into the high coal consumption per gross ton mile on a metre gauge section disclosed an extensive fraud by which coal was diverted illicitly from coal depots to private cotton mills. Some of these enquiries gave me an excuse for leaving office, particularly to use instruments we had obtained for recording vehicle and track vibrations. The catchment enquiry led to my record walk – thirty miles in one day under a tropical sun.

It was probably as a result of this research work that I first became officially acquainted with the Government of India. The first instance was the result of a request that railways should be represented at a meeting to discuss a proposal that Tatas should install a plant in India for the manufacture of steel sleepers. Carew Smythe asked me to attend and I found that I was the only person present who knew much about the subject. One result was that I made a friend of Tata's America consulting Engineer, Perrin. Several times in after years he tried to induce me to work for one of his undertakings but I was not interested. He told Kathleen that I was wasting my time in a backwater - evidently we had different values about living our lives. Quite accidentally he once did me a substantial service. Soon after I had become Agent, Highet, one of our Directors, was visiting India and I had been explaining to him that if he wanted me to entertain Prime Ministers and such like, the Board would have to provide me with a substantial entertainment allowance. We were walking to the bungalow for lunch when a peon interrupted me with a foreign telegram. I read it, laughed and handed it to Highet. It was from Perrin offering me an appointment and asking me to state my terms. It was completely effective so far as the Board were concerned.

The second occasion that I came in contact with the Government of India was towards the end of the war when the Government at last began to consider the revision of the bridge rules. Railways were asked to provide their comments and I contributed an essay, which resulted in me being invited to become a member of a committee to revise the rules. This gave me a lot of work during the next few years including a visit to America on a delegation from government to collect information. The first meeting of the committee was in Simla on Armistice Day. When I had left Secunderabad, the influenza epidemic had just reached us. On my journey I found groups of villagers at places along the line with their sick and dying faces, hoping for help. I wired to Dwane, who was acting for Carew Smythe who was ill, with the result that special trains were hurriedly despatched with all the medical supplies necessary. They gave all the help possible and the service of the railway was greatly appreciated. The next surprise was the Armistice which was announced the night I arrived in Simla. It resulted in absolute pandemonium at the Cecil Hotel where I was staying. The guests, sober officials and their wives, completely lost their heads and behaved like excited children. The hotel management deluged us with champagne and the resulting celebration was something that would never be repeated in Simla. The Bridge Committee pulled itself together next day and held its first meeting."

Not mentioned here was considerable work done for the war effort in the Railway Workshops. Lloyd Jones was also asked to advise on a factory built to manufacture explosives. The problem was that *arak* (native spirit) was one of the ingredients in the manufacture and it was found that the spirit corroded the pipes being used.

In conformity with the requirement of the time, Lloyd Jones rejoined the Volunteers but found that he had to start at the bottom as a private. More should be said about the break in the hot weather at the hill stations. Lloyd Jones himself was only able to get away for two or three weeks but Kathleen and the boys spent the worst of the hot weather in the hills. The hot weather in Secunderabad was not so severe as in North India but nonetheless it was felt that wives and children should be spared its rigours. The most popular and most convenient hills were the Nilgiris in South India. Ootacamund was the queen of the stations but for the early years Kotagiri, being lower down the hill and therefore cheaper, was patronised. It lacked the rolling downs of Ooty, which so reminded the nostalgic of 'home', but was in the forest belt, which had its charms. Flora and fauna were more colourful and many championed Kotagiri over Ooty. For a change and perhaps to savour more gaiety, one hot weather was spent in Mussouri in the Himalaya foothills to the North but generally the Nilgiris were the firm favourites.

Another escape from Secunderabad but not so far away was the annual Christmas Camp. Different sites were chosen – one of the most frequented was Indalwai. Shooting of all kinds of game was the main recreation but much good feasting and drinking accompanied the seasonal good cheer.

Generally the Europeans, although deprived of home leave for a long period, were fortunate to avoid the hardships of the war. Delicacies from England became unobtainable but there was never any food shortage. The men were not subject to conscription and in any case, official policy encouraged them to stay in jobs which were essential for Imperial Defence. Life, in fact, continued relatively untroubled. For most, the anxiety was confined to waiting for news of relatives and friends actually involved in the war. Lloyd Jones' youngest brother, Harold, was severely wounded in France but the family suffered no actual bereavement.

Agent of the Railway

Unfortunately Lloyd Jones' personal account ends in 1919. This is how he concludes. I commenced to write these notes to record the sort of life a civil engineer had in India at the time. I find that it is becoming a sort of a success story and I must explain why this is. I am convinced that my success was mainly due to the training I had received before coming out. The training at the Central was the first example in Britain of teaching technical science to a university standard. I was a new product for India and had little competition. It was not until I was comparatively senior that I began to come across younger men with a training similar to mine. I made innumerable mistakes during my service but they were seldom technical errors."

He started to officiate as Agent when Smythe went on leave in 1919. When he broke the news of the appointment to his wife it was the only time she was left speechless with surprise. It was certainly a remarkable position to arrive at the early age of under 40 and, of course, it meant promotion over the heads of a number of his older colleagues. However, in view of his undoubted ability the advancement appears to have been accepted with good grace.

The position of Agent, despite its rather incongruous sounding title, was one of importance in Hyderabad State ranking perhaps behind the Resident and the General commanding the military district, but unlike them, he was a permanent resident and thereby acquired greater influence through his knowledge of the place and people. Certainly in the matter of emoluments he rose above all others. Starting with Rs 3,500 plus a Rs 500 allowance per month, he soon reached Rs 5000 per month, a very high salary for the time, and all this without income tax. Working in an Indian State, he was not subject to British Indian taxes, although those would not be very severe.

Colonel Smythe had built a truly magnificent residence for the Agent with a garden which had few rivals. He had been an expert rose grower. The Lloyd Joneses lacking this expertise, the roses deteriorated, which caused some muttering among the railway staff who regarded the garden as a sort of pleasure park for their enjoyment. Nevertheless, the gardens as a whole were well maintained with a particularly lush fernery. The house had the usual spacious reception rooms and an effort had been made to provide running hot water. An intending bather had to give advance notice of his intentions and then a stove on the roof just above the bath room was lit with much smoke belching forth and in due course the hot water would come through the tap.

The occupation of this house by the Agent and his family was the source of much joy but it had one disadvantage. Being so comfortable and up to date in its amenities, it was the wish of any one of importance visiting Secunderabad to stay there. Lloyd Jones made mention of this in his request to the Board for an enhanced entertainment allowance. Stories were told of some of the celebrities. During an M.C.C. tour Herbert Sutcliffe was staying. At the same time, an All India Polo Tournament was being held in Secunderabad. Lloyd Jones, whose knowledge of the sporting world was non-existent, mistook his guest for one of the polo stars to the considerable surprise of the celebrated cricketer. Another visitor was Sir Herbert Samuel, a member of the Simon Commission. In order to get some idea of rural life he visited a village, where he remarked on the fact that women were working in the fields leaving their infants at home in a peaceful, even soporific, condition. The Liberal gentleman was shocked to the core when he was informed of the trick, which was for the mother to pop a little opium into the baby's mouth before departing to work.

Apart from visiting V.I.P.s Lloyd Jones found himself in close contact with the top men in Hyderabad State. He had always got on well with Indians. He was an honorary member of the Hyderabad Officers Club and he encouraged Indianization of the staff of the railway. Many are the undoubtedly sincere testimonials written by Indian engineers expressing gratitude for the encouragement and guidance that they had received. Among the Nawabi aristocracy, the relationship was social and it must be said that this class of Indians, never having been subject to the indignity of being under British rule, found it easier to mix on gracious terms without trace of servility on the one hand or bitterness on the other. Lloyd Jones' manner and the charm of his wife made things all the more easy. They never gave the impression that it was a duty to consort with their Indian friends but rather a pleasure.

By far, the closest and most important friendship was with Sir Akbar Hydari, Finance Minister and later Prime Minister of Hyderabad. Not a Hyderabadi himself, he came of a prominent Bombay family, who had entered government service in the Audit Department. He was seconded to the Nizam's Government by the Government of India and he served the State with great distinction for the rest of his career. A highly intelligent and able man, he found in the Englishman an associate with a mind as keen as his own and a genuine desire not only to run a good railway but also to benefit the state and its people. As time went on, the two men worked ever closer together, and through Hydari, the Nizam's Government came to rely on Lloyd Jones' advice and efforts in most technical matters that came up.

Not only were the two men close but their families were very friendly also. Lady Hydari, a remarkable woman in her own right, and her children were frequently entertained by the Joneses. The hospitality was reciprocated by the Hydaris. This friendship lasted all their lives and when in England, Sir Akbar and Lady Hydari always visited the Lloyd

Jones' home in Guildford. Another great friend of the family was Nawab Salar Jung. He owned an extensive collection of antique weapons, armour and objects d'art, both Indian and European, which was always a great attraction for the children. The generosity of the Indians could be embarrassing. One Christmas the children were presented with a whole roomful of toys only to be told to their great distress that the presents would all have to be returned, since they might be regarded as a bribe.

Kathleen and the two boys left for England early in 1919. It was felt essential to get Richard, the eldest boy, into school in England as soon as possible, as his education in India had been inadequate. Lloyd Jones had to stay on in Secunderabad to officiate as Agent but the long period without home leave began to tell on his health. He spent periods confined to bed with fever and at one stage, had to go to hospital. In addition, he was occupied with visits from Colonel Huddleston, Chairman of the London Board and other directors, who were taking the opportunity to go out to India once the end of the war made this possible. It was essential that the officiating Agent should show up well and he took the Board members on extensive tours of the railway system. The Bridge Enquiry Committee was continuing its work which necessitated further visits to Delhi and Simla.

Early in 1920, Lloyd Jones was able to get away on leave. Unfortunately, perhaps due to the change in climate, he developed severe sciatica on arrival in England. At times he was unable to move and Kathleen had to relieve the pain by ironing his back through brown paper. In the meantime, a daughter, Judy, was born and Richard placed in boarding school at Scarborough.

In June, Lloyd Jones left for America on a mission, arranged with the Bridge Committee, to investigate American practice in the matter of railway bridges. Bridge Committee he travelled extensively in the States but this time he had no intention of seeking employment there – he was too firmly and successfully established in India. He did, however, once more take the opportunity to see his various cousins as well as his sister Edith and family in Pennsylvania. On return to England, he did further work for the bridge committee before setting sail for India with his wife, younger son and baby daughter. It was at this time that Lloyd Jones assumed permanently the post of Agent and the family moved into their official residence.

His work was naturally confined for the most part to his office in Secunderabad. He had little or no time for purely engineering work. Rather he was concerned with general administration entailing regular correspondence with the London Board, meetings with the Nizam's authorities and contacts with the Government of India. Finance occupied much attention and with his mathematical turn of mind he showed an ability which was to enhance his reputation with the shareholders. Once or twice a year he went out on line inspections. This inspection tour in the train was far grander than the tour of the District Engineer of the old days. The whole train was made up of saloons for the various members of the staff. The Agent himself had a splendid saloon – this had separate dining and drawing rooms, two bedrooms with essential offices on an appropriate scale. At the rear of the train was an inspection coach, open at the back and with seats arranged so that the engineers could inspect the track as the train progressed. On the front of the engine, a bench was fixed which could also be used for inspection as the train puffed its way across the Deccan plateau. On one occasion, the train rounding a curve ran into a buffalo on the line, splashing the engineers with blood and entrails. But generally, a ride on the front of the engine was a most exhilarating exercise. Lloyd Jones took his young son, Michael, then aged seven, on one of these inspection tours. While it was such a thrilling experience for the boy that the memory of it would always remain with him, the engineers on the train rather deprecated a serious affair being turned into a kiddy's outing.

Visitors of importance were taken to see the famous rock temples of Ajanta and Ellora where the whole architecture including the statuary had been carved out of the solid rock. The most imposing, the temple of Kailas, was almost of cathedral proportions chiselled into the cliff face. Close by was the other great tourist attraction of Daulatabad Fort. Built on top of a hill rising sheer from the plain, it is reputed never to have been captured save through treachery. It was a famous stronghold throughout the Muslim period and for a time was the capital of the Tughlak Empire. The climb to the big cannon at the top was a good test of sightseers' fitness. The more portly or decrepit were hauled up the hill in palanquins. Among the visitors at this time were the American cousins, Edward Jones and his sister, Jeanette. For other personages a tiger shoot was considered to be necessary. It was arranged that Sir Robert Highet, the Managing Director of the Railway, should bag his first tiger. Another elaborate shoot was laid on for an American party, the Stuyvasants. Social activities played an ever increasing part in the Agent's life and these included dinners and receptions given by the Nizam and the Resident.

In 1923, he took leave in England and this time was free from all official duties. The second son was sent off to boarding school and in

October, the youngest daughter, Rachael was born. The parents cleverly spaced the births of their children so that as one was sloughed off, another appeared to take its place.

Back in India in 1924, Lloyd Jones was asked to arbitrate between the Bombay Port Trust and two of the main railways on terminal charges at the port. This necessitated going to Bombay on several occasions to hear evidence. The dispute was over the rates charged by the Port, which the railways thought excessive and a deterrent to traffic. Lloyd Jones made an equitable decision but also recommended how the Port Trust could increase their efficiency and thereby bring down their costs.

At this time he was offered the post of member of the Railway Board in Delhi. This was an important position with extensive scope and variety of interests. He was undoubtedly tempted but he felt he could not afford the drop in salary that it would have meant. In fact, there was probably no post on Indian railways which would have paid as much as he was getting and his employers had seen to it that he would not be induced to leave the Nizam's Railway for financial reasons.

In Secunderabad, Kathleen had taken on the additional task of Commissioner of Girl Guides. Her daily life was already full with social activities. The steady stream of visitors meant much organization. A large staff of competent servants looked after the actual menial work but everything had to be carefully supervised. Dinners, tennis and children's parties filled the calendar throughout the cold weather months. Entertainment had become more sophisticated since pre-war days. The gramophone had taken the place of private solo efforts, bridge and mahjong had become popular as evening games and the cinema had taken the place, to a large extent, of amateur dramatics. This period reflected in a shadowy form the hectic social life of the contemporary jazz age in Europe and America. Home leave was more frequent than in the earlier years which meant a more up to date following of fashion and taste.

A high point in the social calendar was the visit of the Prince of Wales. For the railway it was very much a repetition of the visit of his father in 1906 which has already been described. The railway line had to be carefully surveyed and the track elaborately patrolled when the royal train passed. The train being longer than the usual express train, some doubt arose as to whether the N.S.R. locomotive was strong enough to pull it and the British Indian railway which had been hauling the train as far as the Hyderabad border, recommended that their engine should continue the journey. This was rejected with indignation by the N.S.R. Nevertheless some tense moments were experienced climbing a stiff gradient on the line. Socially the visit did not quite have the glamour of its predecessor – lacking the glitter of a Princess of Wales covered in diamonds. The Prince, in fact, spent most of his time playing polo. At the Residency Ball some offence was occasioned when the Prince insisted on dancing with a few of the pretty 'young things' instead of taking on the senior memsahibs.

In 1925, Lloyd Jones was chosen to preside over the Indian Railway Conference Association in Simla. This was the coordinating body for all the railways in India and being comparatively young and head of a less important railway system, it was a marked personal distinction to become president. His address was on the subject of cooperation between the railways in matters of joint concern. In particular he stressed the advisability of coordinating the rates and fares structure. Among other things, he pointed out that third class fares in India were the cheapest in the world. Those who have seen how third class passengers travel in India may not be surprised. Bulging out of sparsely furnished carriages, some might say that they should be paid, and not pay, to travel in such discomfort. Mention was made of agitation from some quarters to improve amenities but, in reality, in a poor country cheapness was the main consideration and as far as harsh conditions were concerned, they were better than on some Balkan railways of the period, where cattle trucks with only straw on the floor were provided for the fourth class. Sir Clement Hindley, Commissioner of Railway, complimented the speaker with the words, "There has rarely, perhaps, in the history of the Conference Association been an address so full of constructive suggestions."

At this time, Lloyd Jones became more involved in the construction of new lines. It presented an opportunity to get out of his office into the countryside, which he loved, and where bridges had to be built, he was even more interested. Hyderabad State was one of the few parts of India, for that matter anywhere in the world, which required an extension of the railway network and where construction work was still being carried out. The Nizam's Government was particularly insistent that railways be pushed into undeveloped areas and undoubtedly the building of a railway could transform the agriculture and economy of a region. The improved transport of produce to a wide market would mean the difference between cash crop cultivation and subsistence farming. Parts of Deccan were suitable for cotton growing but this would only be economic when it could be exported to the mills of Gujarat and Bombay cheaply. In addition, the provision of a railway to small towns would allow the expansion of trade and industry.

The line that was being built from 1926 onwards was from Kazipet to Balharshah and was an important link in north south communications. It would generate traffic from outside the state and would clearly be profitable. This could not be said, however, of all the projects which Nizam's Government proposed and here there could be a conflict of interest with the Company. It should be explained that the only line actually owned by the Company was the main line running from Wadi on the Great Indian Peninsular Railway through Secunderabad and Kazipet to join up with the Madras Railway in the south. All other branch lines and extensions were owned by the state but operated by the Company. Even so, it was the main line which contributed the bulk of the profits and the Company was reluctant to operate an extended mileage without much commercial gain. This conflict of interest, though never serious, produced to some extent the reasons for major changes in the future.

Lloyd Jones, although principally a servant of the Company, was through his friendship with Sir Akbar Hydari, sensitive to the interests of the Nizam's Government and sought to reconcile the conflict. His solution was to develop road transport, not in competition with the railway, as elsewhere, but as an adjunct. The idea was to provide railway owned bus and lorry services to bring traffic into railhead. It was obviously cheaper to use existing roads than to construct new lines. A fleet of buses was brought from the U.K. and the Sentinel steam wagons, a sort of road train was also tried with a traction engine pulling a string of trailers for carrying raw cotton. The main restriction on this excellent idea, which was in advance of its time, was the condition of the roads which were the responsibility of the state and not the railway to maintain.

During this period of the late twenties the railway benefited from the worldwide boom that was taking place. Prosperity was in the air and schemes for development and expansion abounded. This is reflected in the Company Report read by the Chairman at the annual general meeting in 1928. He was able to declare a dividend of 16% and this when most railway shareholders were lucky to get 5% only. He said that this fine result had been achieved by modernizing equipment to provide more efficient running and at the same time to carry an increased volume of traffic. He concluded by giving praise where it was due to the Agent and his staff. A stockholder, Mr Frederick Palmer, senior partner in the firm of consulting engineers, Rendel, Palmer & Tritton, moved a resolution thanking the staff and adding, "I want to associate with this resolution the name of Mr Lloyd Jones whose efforts are absolutely continuous, almost day and night." As for the efficient running of the railway, it was pointed out that operating expenses were only 36% of revenue, which was about half the rate on British railways.

In 1930, Lloyd Jones was approached to act as reporter and to read a paper, along with Sir Ashley Biggs, Agent of the Madras and Southern Mahratta Railway, to the International Railway Congress in Madrid. This organization had its headquarters in Brussels and at that time was dominated by French interests. The British representative, anxious to assert English speaking influence, proposed a subject for discussion in which the French had little interest, namely 'penetration railway'. These were new railways built in undeveloped countries and when the Government of India was asked to supply reporters, Lloyd Jones was an obvious choice. The procedure was to circulate interested railways throughout the world with a questionnaire and compile a report from the answers. In fact much of Lloyd Jones' experience comes into it and deals mainly with technical subjects such as the type of track, gauge, alignment, equipment, signalling and so forth. However, one interesting statement of principle appears, that on purely commercial grounds the construction of the railway may not be justified, yet it may provide disproportionate benefits to the community as a whole. "The dividend a railway pays on its capital is not a measure of the service it gives to the community and if the net revenue is insufficient to warrant its construction, there seems no fundamental objection to transferring some part of the burden to others who benefit from its existence." Surely the same principle applies today. Although no new railways are being built, the running of existing lines is often unprofitable and yet the community benefits from its existence and should, therefore, be prepared to subsidize the railway.

A Tour Diary

Seeming to be occupied with prestigious conferences and meetings with important people, staying in first class hotels, travelling in de luxe trains and ocean liners to Europe and all over India, yet Lloyd Jones was quite ready, even eager, for the sudden contrast of roughing it in the jungles and remoter regions of Hyderabad State. There follows a tour diary (probably addressed to his wife) when surveying a projected line from Aurangabad to Udgir in the North Western part of the State during the cold weather of 1930.

Paithan 7-12-30

"We have just arrived at our first camp which is on the Godavari, some

30 miles from Aurangabad, by a good road. We came by motor in under two hours as there was nothing to investigate on the way. The prepared line follows the road, serving the important villages, and the country is easy, presenting no engineering difficulties.

I have sighed with contentment at once more being in the jungle and free from social demands. Even the oil lamps, canvas bath and camp cot have their attractions and it is pleasant to hear the people round the camp fires, the odour of burning wood and the commotion while the motors and horses are being put away for the night. Admittedly the lights are bad, the cooking crude and the appointments not of the best, but I am not too old to appreciate the atmosphere it implies.

I arranged to travel light – only three small tents – but we run to three small cars and two lorries as well as ponies kindly lent by Osman from his cavalry regiment. I find we have about forty people travelling with us but this is partly due to the Survey Engineer's camp, as he is travelling with us, in addition to the Traffic Canvasser who carried out the traffic investigation. He is a most intelligent man, a Brahmin, who had all the details of the traffic of this district at his finger tips.

The moon is coming up–nearly full–we shall be in bed soon after 9 p.m. and Shaffter, the Survey Engineer, demands that we shall do a thirty mile ride in the morning.

I was sorry to leave Secunderabad as I had just become really interested in the work. I had three most interesting subjects in hand, gauge policy, coal consumption and road services. They may sound dull but all are full of interest and mean just getting the details. Luckily Nanda arrived and reported for duty. As they had nothing lined up for him, I got him put on special duty for my work. I have now left him working up details, promising to return and work with him during Christmas week. He was quite agreeable.

Bill Walker is my only companion. I had to make Shaffter understand quite plainly that he must run a separate camp. I could stand him for a few days but several weeks of Shaffter was more than I could stand. However he quite understands and is a very valuable man, on friendly terms with most of the officials. You may have heard me mention Bill Walker's faculty for inventing thing – usually quite useless things like pillows and razor sharpeners. But some of this inventions are useful and he has made several thousand pounds out of them, so they are not entirely humorous, although most of them are. He is busy now trying to make some petrol lamps work. I am writing by the light of one of them and it is not quite as good as the ordinary hurricane lantern.

It was rather hot travelling up from Secunderabad yesterday and I am afraid I was angry several times at idiotic working. At no less than three stations the train stopped several hundred yards short of the platform and disgorged its passengers in the dark amongst sidings, because the driver took a fancy to watering somewhere where there were no facilities. We slept in the saloon in Aurangabad yard and were partly devoured by sand flies. I was not in the best of tempers in the morning and to make matters worse I found the waiting room occupied by our camp clerk and the rest house lent to two men from Bombay. I started off to evict the latter but on striding into a room found some lady's underclothing laid neatly over a chair, so retired in confusion.

I called on the Taluqdar (commissioner) at Aurangabad in the afternoon– Vikar ud din – a very pleasant man but on the subject of railways he had the mind of a child. Aurangabad suggests that the people are living in a ruined city. There must have been fine buildings and palaces at one time but its glory has departed and now it is mostly dust heaps.

The Tehsildar (local government official) of Paithan called on me this evening. He is a young Muslim, name Mohamed Ansari, educated at the– boarding house and the Ujain College. He speaks excellent English and seems most intelligent. He arranged to take me round his town in the morning but showed some hesitation as smallpox is raging. I don't suppose I shall come to any harm walking through the streets.

Walker and I are greatly impressed by the courtesy of every one we meet. Of course, the officials would be polite but all along the road from Aurangabad to Paithan nearly every passer-by *salaamed* and several got out of their carts or off their ponies to do it. When we stopped, as we did several times to verify the names of villages and the cart tracks, the people were most friendly and affable.

Shahgadh 8-12-30

Not a very good day. Shaffter thought he would save us part of the thirty mile ride and therefore we made a preliminary journey by car to a village to which the horses had been sent. We were so late in arriving by car, however, that there was insufficient time to do any work on the ride to camp. We decided therefore to drive on to our camp at Shahgadh and to return tomorrow by car and do the work we should have done today. It is annoying because we have had a long motor ride over country we are not obliged to see and have lost a day.

The day started well. I walked down to the river and exposed a few feet on the scene of activity (cine film)–streams of people and animals bringing water to the town. All kinds of utensils, brass pots in trays hanging round a bullock, two large pots on a donkey, pots in carts and carried by women. I hope the photograph comes out well. The Tehsildar then took us round the town and in particular he showed me the buildings he was clearing and digging out the river silt. One of them he assured me was a palace built by Shalimar, a Maharatta prince who lived at Deogir and raided as far north as Bengal, long before the Moghul invasion. I took this on trust but Michael is the historian and may be able to verify this. Anyhow Ansari had found a stair which led to a chamber in the rock which we inspected. I was not clear what the place was. It was well executed and decorated, so possibly it could have been a prison.

I had a long talk with Ansari and the following is more or less what he told me. The population and importance of Paithan was declining steadily. Until recently, there had been a prosperous industry –*saris* and *puggaris* (turbans) which were decorated with gold thread. The craft had now quite ceased, not entirely due to competition but also to the decreased use of expensive articles of the kind. The principal market was Gujarat where now the Gandhi cap had almost entirely replaced the puggari. A railway would save Paithan.

There was a lot of communal trouble in the district but the villagers did not identify the Nizam with their enemies or with the Muslim officials. In Paithan and in other Maratha villages, the villagers worshipped Mahboob Ali Khan, the late Nizam, as a saint and had erected a tomb in his honour. The villagers took no interest in politics except here and there where some agent from British India had been able to steal through and talk to them. The people I spoke to were very friendly and when I asked about the fish in the river, a man produced two small *mahsair* - just caught.

The motor drive was not very interesting. The route we took was Paithan, Dawarwari, Wilkamander, Pimpalgaon, Mahankal and Shahgadh. We saw several herds of buck, some quite close and with good heads. I finished a spool of film. The country was so flat and there were many people in the standing crops, so that it would have been dangerous to fire. We met a fine looking old Pathan at Pimpalgaon who talked with us for a time and directed us on our way. I hear he is a moneylender who has practically the whole village under his thumb.

I am now waiting for dinner and Bill Walker is wandering about in the scrub with a gun. He has the lamp of an electric torch clamped to his forehead and the batteries stuffed in his shirt and expects to put up some thing–I cant think what – but I hope he fires the other way.

Shahgadh 9-12-30

We are at the same camp and have returned from our first ride. We motored this morning to Wilkamander and rode back to camp via Hiradpuri and Pimpalgaon. This was the route but we left it from time to time to visit villages or get a better view of the country. We halted some time at Hiradpur and had lunch and walked up the river, so we did not reach camp until about five. I was somewhat stiff and felt much better after a swim in the river. The current was just a bit more powerful than my efforts and after about fifteen minutes hard swim, I found myself 100 yards downstream. But it was very pleasant.

I exposed about 40 feet of film today on several good subjects – vultures on a carcass, ploughing, smiths at work on a cartwheel and a religious ceremony on the Godavari. The latter was quite interesting. There is a curious rock barrier across the river at Hiradpur with a gap about 100 feet wide through which the river passes when not in flood. The gap must be deep as the flow is slow. There were marks on the rocks of red paint, offerings of food and money, so it was evidently a sacred spot. While we were discussing lunch under a tree on the bank, a party arrived in two carts. It consisted of six women each with a very young infant, one or two old men and a few children. They were met by two priests and two men with drums, who escorted them to the rocks and performed some kind of ceremony, which we watched through our glasses. After a time each baby in turn was placed in a small cot or cradle which floated on chatties (earthenware pots) and the baby was pushed out in the stream – escorted by two men swimming – until it reached the opposite side of the gap. It was then pushed back and received in the arms of an obviously anxious mother. Usually the infant yelled vigorously the whole time. We were informed that the idea was that the mother gave the child to Ganga (the holy river) who in due course returned it to her. Anyhow it was a pretty ceremony and I hope the pictures come out well.

The ride was uneventful and the ponies were quite comfortable. We picked up *bigaris* at each village who conducted us to the next and we had porters carrying guns, rifle, water, tiffin, camera, plans and instruments, so we could not travel very fast. We had some good canters, however, when we left the route and also for the last four miles when we left our people behind. I shall feel the effects tomorrow. This is quite a good camp on a high bank of the Godavari overlooking the ford, which is sufficiently far away to make the noise of the cartmen unobjectionable as they encourage and abuse their teams.

Tomorrow we cross the river and halt at Gevrai on the way to Bir. The motors all went across today. They must have been nearly submerged as the river is 3 ft. 6 in. deep at one place. They removed all the electrical equipment and have now refixed it and reported that all five cars are in good order on the far bank.

Bill Walker seems to have suffered somewhat from his ride. He had trouble with his stirrups and told me of a scheme he intended to work out by which his stirrups would be on springs and adjust themselves to his requirements. He shifted uneasily on his saddle as we were picking our way into camp and asked me whether I thought it possible to stuff saddles with sponge rubber.

Gevrai 10-12-30

We had a ride of about 20 miles today and arrived in camp for tiffin. I was sufficiently tired to enjoy a slack during the afternoon but the camp is badiy situated without any shade and between three roads. It was very hot in our small tents.

We had a long talk to the people of Dhondari village who were very friendly and affable. This village also is declining in importance and population. They say they pay Rs 40,000 in taxes but they don't seem to get much for it – no roads or drains – hardly a building worth the name and great difficulty about water. It would cost very little to give them a water system, put their streets and drains in order and generally clear up. It seems to me that the Maharatta is having a bad time and they seem to be a really good type of people. Perhaps something will happen when we go. Certainly the ruined buildings in nearly every village leads one to suppose that they must have been more prosperous in the past. They say the grain and seed crops are satisfactory but the cotton practically a failure. About half the grain goes to Jalna and of the balance, half to Ahmednagar and half consumed locally. Prices are falling rapidly everywhere. The prices of grain and *ghee* are said to be lower than they have been for 30 years.

The Taluqdar of Bir, Zain Yar Jung, called at the camp and announced all manner of dinners and parties for us at Bir, which make my spirits fall. I remember the man once at Simla but cannot recollect the circumstances. He had a brother who was Accountant General in Sir Reginald Glancy's time, Habibullah something. I expect I will hear more about him later. We leave for Bir tomorrow.

Bir 12-12-30

The last two days have been marred by infernal functions which the Taluqdar has prepared in our honour. Yesterday we arrived in camp late about 6 p.m. and the official reception had been fixed for 5 p.m. I insisted on a bath and change as I had been out all day and we did not arrive at the show until 7 p.m. They did not seem to mind and we were received in a square lighted by high power lamps and lined by officials and principal citizens. Behind was a rabble I could only hear and smell but not see. After being introduced to the outskirts of the throng and expressing my apologies to the Taluqdar, we took our seats in the centre and the Taluqdar called upon the Nazim for an ode. He explained to me that the Nazim was a great poet.

The Nazim, an elderly Muslim, dressed in a sherwani and fez, with a pock marked face then proceeded to intone an Urdu poem. Slight as is my knowledge of Urdu, curiously enough I managed to understand quite a lot of it and the Taluqdar helped me out when I was in trouble. It was evidently very flowery but the general idea was that he enumerated the glories of Bir in the past and asked why they did not endure. He spoke of the princes and rulers who had reigned and lived in Bir, the merchants who had grown wealthy, and the peasants who had prospered. Where now were the palaces – in ruins, where the wealthy merchants – impoverished and the peasants found it difficult to live. The palaces were in ruins, the gardens overgrown with weeds and the craftsmen idle. Why had this come to pass? Were the rulers less able – no. Were the merchants less enterprising – no. Had the men of Marathwara degenerated – no (prolonged cheers). Then what was the cause of their downfall? It was that Bir was no longer a trade centre. Trade no longer moved by road but by rail and the centre of trade had moved to the railway. Bring a railway to Bir and Bir would live again and today was one for rejoicing, because where Lloyd Jones Sahib Bahadur came one year, the rail would come the next, and he was here. If a railway came to Bir, his name would remain forever in the memory of its citizens – and a lot more to the same effect. Every couplet was greeted with cheers or groans from the assembly, according to its purport.

The Taluqdar then called upon the Munsif (judge) for an effort and I had more difficulty with him. He was a very stout man with spectacles and a walking stick with silver knob. He was obviously a humorist and every sentence was greeted with shouts of laughter. He must have been funny, because I found him most amusing, although I could only get the *general drift of his remarks. He intoned his poem in Urdu, repeating the first line of each couplet. It was a kind of satirical description of life in Bir, to which he had been transferred only recently. He described the housing problem, the roads, the bus service to Jalna, the postal service and so on, having a satirical comment on each. He then proceeded to appreciate the benefits of the present Taluqdar, Zain Yar Jung, and said that now their greatest hope was in Lloyd Jones Sahib. It was not on account of his manly beauty (he interpolated a remark that I would not understand what he was saying) but because he was a builder of railways and would not be there unless he meant business.

We then exchanged *salaams* with each of the guests and the Taluqdar escorted us to his bungalow where we eventually dined. I wish I could adequately describe the little crowd of officials at the reception. They are common enough types in Hyderabad – I don't know if they are elsewhere – and I think they are most attractive. Probably most of them are frightful rogues but very pleasant ones. The dinner was an ordeal– about fifteen courses all very dull imitations of English dishes except a curry which was very bad. The Taluqdar entertained us with accounts of his prowess either as a hunter, a horseman, an administrator – even details of his ancient lineage. I find most Indians do this sort of thing and I suppose from their point of view it is not bad form but it always sounds odd to me.

I attended an at home this afternoon and met most of the same people again. The Taluqdar started off by asking me to read a printed pamphlet containing letters of various people, who had written in praise of him. We had tea and then had our photographs taken. I took a few cine pictures of the guests.

It sounds as though we had spent all our time being entertained but actually we have been working hard. Yesterday we motored some 60 miles and were out all day examining Balaghat. Today we were out from 7 a.m. until 3 p.m. without lunch examining Pipalgaon Ghat. Bir town is on the north side of the Bir plateau – on the low ground – and the problem with which we are now concerned and which will occupy us for the next week is to find the best way of bringing the railway up onto the plateau from the north. Bir is about 1700 feet above sea level and the plateau about 2400 feet, so we have to rise 700 feet at least but actually 800 feet from where we are. The declivity between the Bir plateau and the Godavari plain below to the north consists of steep hills cut up by valleys and ravines and we have to explore this for a railway route. It is a misnomer to call the edge of the plateau a cliff, because it is too broken, but if you think of it as such, we have to examine a cliff about 100 miles long. It is called the Balaghat Range. We have started at the western end and will work along to the east. Today and yesterday, we have examined about 15 miles of it, of course, only superficially but sufficiently to get an idea of the possibilities and the difficulties. It is very heavy work on foot and very slow with a lot of climbing. I find very useful a pair of rock climbing boots I bought at great expense in Aberdeen. I find the spikes just right and although the boots are heavy, they are none too heavy for the work. The motors are most useful as the top of the hill is a flat plain and motors can go anywhere – dead slow over small boulders – and it saves a lot of energy. When we have had to get into another valley, we have found it quicker to climb to the head of the valley, get into the motors and drive round to the next valley. Luckily we have excellent maps and the hills are bare of jungle, so having got to a point of vantage, we examine the valley with glasses. We then hold a conference to decide at what levels we could traverse the valley, at what cost and with what curves we could turn.

We move camp early tomorrow to a place 20 miles further along the foot of the cliff and start afresh. This has been a good camp at Bir. It is in an old Mogul garden full of very old and large mango tress. It is dusk even at midday. They tried to make us occupy the Dak bungalow (rest house), which had been specially prepared but I struck. The Taluqdar said the garden camping ground was full of snakes. I said I liked snakes, so they gave in. Had they cut out their infernal functions, I should have enjoyed Bir but these dinners are the devil and I have another tonight. The only consolation is that our cook is drunk and we might not have had much of a dinner in camp. But we are well supplied. The Talukdar sent us two haunches of venison and baskets of fruit. Bill shot a pea fowl and we obtained very good vegetables in the town.

There were literally hundreds of buck round us today. I had left my rifle and camera in camp so that I should not waste time. Two or three herds raced the cars only a few hundred feet away and crossed in front of us. It's bad luck because I wanted a good photograph of a herd and I shall never get a better chance. We are still stiff from riding, although we have not ridden for the last two days. However, we have lots of chance ahead of us as we are abandoning motor transport for the next 100 miles and sending it along the plateau to meet us at the other end in about a week's time. In the meantime, we have to rely on our horses and on bullock carts for the luggage.

I am just about to drink as much whiskey as I can before departing to the Taluqdar's banquet, which will be a T.T. show as he is a strict Muslim.

Katiawari 14-12-30

I have more or less recovered from the stiffness from riding but I cannot bend my face. It is so sunburnt that it is brittle and most uncomfortable. However, we are clear of the gaieties of Bir which is a blessing. We have an addition to our camp of two mounted police and three unmounted. I was glad to have the mounted men because they ride forward to villages and get *bigaris* ready but I did not want the footsloggers. But the Taluqdar would not take no for on answer and explained that it was almost indecent to go about without them, so I agreed. They mount guard round the camp with fixed bayonets and look most impressive.

The Survey Engineer apparently did himself too well at the Taluqdar's banquets and has been very sorry for himself the last few days. In consequence, we are making shorter marches. We did 20 miles yesterday, 15 miles today and propose to do only 10 miles tomorrow. A march of 20 miles is far too long as it keeps us out from sunrise to sunset. We have to cover much more than the route mileage. Yesterday's camp was very poor but as we only used it to sleep in, it did not matter. This camp is better but gives too much prominence to the servants' tents. We have a man always a camp ahead who selects the sites and in time we shall get him to fix good sites. He has had a rotten time whenever we have come up with him but he is improving. He now understands that we do not like camping on the village green or on the village drain. He is also beginning to realize that we want shade. We have now to convince him that much as we appreciate our entourage, we do not like the servants' tents in the middle of the camp.

We have had some pleasant talks with the Mahrata villagers. They are very attractive people, most polite and respectful. The headmen of the villages always come out to greet us and if we rest, anyone near invariably comes up, squats down and begins to talk. At several villages, the people have told us that we are the first Europeans they remember coming there and they themselves seem to travel very little. The roads are dreadful and the going has been very hard the last few days – either rock or covered with small boulders. It is very bad for the ponies. The way they clamber in and out of nullahs has surprised me. My mare is as clever as a cat and never stumbles. She is always willing to break into a canter whenever we get a reasonably good stretch of ground and she walks considerably faster than a man. Unfortunately apart from the bad surface, we cannot travel fast because we are dependent on our guides who are not mounted. However, we change them every few miles and they keep up fairly well if we are not too exacting.

Nagapur 16-12-30

We have finished our bread but the cook's *chapatis* are good and he has produced some beef he bought at Gevrai and has salted on the march. It is excellent. We have really done very well so far. Two days on venison and pea fowl and now salted beef and sand grouse. Our midday lunch we take with us and it usually consists of excellent curry puffs, *chapatis*, cheese and hard boiled eggs. Then some oranges, apples and bananas. I have no complaints about the servants.

We have had hard marches the last few days. We found the ponies could not stand the country. They had lost four shoes between them and one was very slightly lame – she is all right now. In consequence we decided to rest them and walk for two days. Unfortunately I was not dressed for walking; I had a cloth suit and lightish boots. The boots gave out very early and a nail came through the heel and I started a hole in my heel and several blisters. However, I staggered into camp at Kajanpur with the help of my long bamboo. Today was much better; I had the Scotch boots, thick socks and light khaki clothes, so I could camp at Nagapur quite fresh. The work has not been very interesting, as the line located presents no difficulty and none of the *ghats* were worth examining. We have a short march to Purli tomorrow, where I hope our motor transport awaits us. We shall probably be two days at Purli and will then have a 16 mile climb up the *ghat* which our Survey Engineer believes to be the most suitable for the line.

We got a *dak* (post) from Purli when we arrived in camp. The only paper of interest was the English mail. It is nearly 12 days since I received the previous letter.

Purli 17-12-30

We walked in here today and found our motors waiting for us. Unfortunately one car had broken down with a broken Carden shaft bearing. We are now at a railway station and have wired for a new bearing. We are also having the ponies shod and are taking the day off on our mail. Several of the men are down with fever including my own man, Nursimloo, who always accompanies me. To complete the sad tale, I find that the colour filter on my camera has developed a blister and I have wired to Bombay for a spare filter. We shall be here two days and our next two camps will be easily accessible by motor and so I hope we shall patch up our men and material without trouble.

Chakur 22-1230

I last wrote at Purli and we are now four marches further. The first two in the *ghats* and the last two on the plateau–the former very strenuous and the latter long but simple. This camp is on the Nander–Chakur road – a new road over the Godavari across a new bridge and connecting with our station at Nander. It is a pleasant camp in a mango grove but we have not been able to appreciate it much as we arrived about sunset.

We spent two days at Purli. The second day we motored on a good road to Kalain. It was a long drive. We went to see what the country was like and we saw continuous plains of cultivation; *jawar* (millet), cotton, wheat and linseed – not an acre uncultivated. We saw herds of buck but I took no photographs as the colour filter has given out.

On the following day we started an inspection of the *ghat*. We have to rise 500 feet in 10 miles and Shaffter, the Survey Engineer, has located a line and we had to vet it. We took with us his plans and sections, the latter being contoured to 5 ft intervals. The line has been pegged out. The procedure was as follows: *kallaris* (rod men) went ahead with long surveying rods and placed them on the pegs. We could then view about a mile of line ahead. We would then have the plans laid out and discuss the alignment. You must understand that we were among the hills which are cut up by steep ravines and the line winds in and out of the ravines along the hill side. A movement of the line only a few feet to the right or left meant an entire change in the cross section and modified it on the next section also. It was slow work but most interesting and we were able to find many ways of improving the alignment. We could do nothing final but we have given Shaffter enough work to carry him on for another few weeks and left him behind to worry it out. We took two days over the ten miles; even then we were out from sunrise to sunset – very strenuous work climbing along the hill side, in and out of ravines. Most of the nails have come out of the Aberdeen boots but they have done me very well. Our first camp was at Chandapur, a little village in the hills and the second at Ghat Nander, a big village at the top of the *ghat*. The motors and horses went round by road.

Shaffter's general route is admirable. There are several places where we can get from the 1700 ft contour to 2100 ft contour but Purli as at 1500 ft. Shaffter gets to the foot of the hills at 1550 ft and has found a valley and hill which just fit the 5 degree curve to which we are working, so that he turns 180 degrees in the valley and back again 180 degrees round the hill rising to 1650 ft. We are then restricted to a hill between two valleys and run up one side about 8 miles across ravines and through spurs. It appears to be the only practicable route with the restriction of a one per cent grade and five degree curve. We saw nothing on the hills of interest except sand grouse – no deer and very little vegetation. I was intensely interested in the location problem but apart from that I was glad to leave the barren hillsides and get onto country one could ride over. There are so many problems on a *ghat* location – when to cut, tunnel or cut and cover–how to cross ravines, fills, masonry or steel – how to get spoil for fills and what sort of a section one could get in cuts.

We had a good camp at Ghat Nander and joined our horses and motors. Shaffter left us and one of his surveyors, Damodaram, took us to Chakur. He showed us an excellent piece of location but, of course, the country is easy. Our procedure was much the same except there were few matters for criticism, usually a few curves can be eased or removed or the line shifted to avoid a plantation or well. The general line was not in question. We examined the plans well before starting and the plans and sections are pinned to drawing boards and carried by *kallaris.* The surveying rods are sent out and we go steadily over the line mile by mile. It was mostly through standing crops and ploughed fields and we managed to average 3 miles per hour. We rode the first day and our camp was pitched at Paugaon, giving us a march of only 10 miles. We found it much too short as we reached there at about 2 p.m. However, it was very pleasant and we had plenty of office work to occupy us in the afternoon. Also the *dak* arrived with the Christmas mail by motor from Purli, so we were quite happy. Today we had a march of 22 miles, walked the first 11 miles, had lunch under a tree and rode in the afternoon arriving about 5.30. Our transport moves by lorry and takes only three hours. It was a pleasant day, quite cool but of little technical interest. The crops are magnificent and we saw hardly an acre of uncultivated ground. We were pleased to accede to every request from villagers to avoid their wells and plantations. Some of the hills looked interesting but we had no time to climb up them. One or two touched 2500 ft and appeared to have temples on top. I hope they will be able to have a few rest houses or sanatoria up here when the line is opened as the elevation is some 700 ft above Secunderabad. We are now quite used to the ordeal of walking and riding and cease to suffer. I have some raw places on my ankles but they do not worry me. My face is still rather corrugated but I have obtained a tube of lanoline which will probably cure it. Unfortunately last night the light was not too good and I found this morning I had rubbed on tooth paste by mistake but I don't suppose it did any harm.

Most of the way has been through standing crops and the *jawar* must be 8 ft high. The place for lunch happened to be near a chilli field and a handful of green chillis came in very well and enabled us for the first time to consume all of our sandwiches. The cook is doing very well, salting beef and tongue and making curry puffs. Bill Walker takes very ill to the sort of lunch we carry, sandwiches, eggs, cheese and curry puffs and fruit. The water in canvas bags keeps icy cold and we drink it with lime juice. It is excellent.

I have had two grave disappointments. Kodaks have sent me a neutral density filter in reply to my wire instead of a colour filter, so the camera cannot be used. Also Rosenthal said he had no written instruction about going on with the bungalow and has taken no action, whereas I expected the roof to be off and the place ready for me to occupy when I return on the 26th. I have now instructed them to carry on but it means that I cannot occupy it when I go into Secunderabad. Our Engineering Department seems to be designed to do everything except engineering work. I was too disgusted for words.

We are now waiting dinner for the unfortunate Wilkinson. We arranged that he should come here by car from Purli with some tenders and it is now 8.30 p.m. and he has not arrived. We shall now have dinner and he will probably spend the night in the car It will be an experience for him.

I came upon a strange crop today. We found a few small patches of it near villages and could not ascertain what it was except that it is call *bhainsa*. At last some people told us that it is grown for the village women who use it as a hair wash. It might be a commercial success if properly advertised.

Utgir 23-12-30

Wilkinson did not turn up last night but one of the cars came in from Purli and brought me a tube of stuff for my face and the news that Wilkinson was not coming until today. We have now pushed on another 20 miles, so he will have his work cut out to reach us. Having gone 200 miles north, he will have to motor about the same distance back and probably catch us at Secunderabad from where he started. We are camped in Noorjehan's garden at Utgir. I believe she was the daughter of Shahjahan but I am not sure. (actually she was the famous wife of Jahangir). She built a sort of summerhouse in the garden and we are camped round it. The summerhouse is a three storied building and Bill Walker proposes to live in it while he is building the line. It is a very pleasant camp though, as we arrived late, we have not seen much of it. I propose to keep this camp for about ten days, as I now have to go to Secunderabad to dispose of very necessary office work and will return here after Christmas. The second camp will be pitched at Bidar.

This morning we had a ride of about 10 miles round Chakur looking at two alternative lines. One is above the town and gives an excellent station site. The other is below the town; it is a shorter and cheaper alignment but I doubt whether it is a suitable site for what may be an important station and junction. We had lunch in camp and moved after lunch. It is the second sit down lunch we have had in camp, all the others being sandwiches and this was a welcome change. Afterwards we walked over the line for three hours and then motored on to this camp. We shall return later to walk over the rest of the line. We have got on to the construction staff now and Balakrishna, the Assistant Engineer, is busy overhauling the alignment and it is this work we have to examine and discuss. He is a very good type of Indian Engineer. He started with us as a tracer and has been trained entirely on our line, with no previous training at an engineering college but he has read and learnt in the evenings at the local technical institute. He knows all about his job and gets work done cheaper, quicker and better than most of our assistant engineers. The last two constructions we did entirely with similar staff and they were very successful.

Bill Walker is busy improving his saddlery. He has invented a cleat he is fixing to his saddle to tie up his reins. He says it is silly to hold them all the time when you are just going straight and also a cleat is useful to hook up the reins if the horse is bolting. Tomorrow we shall motor to Bidar where I shall spend Christmas day. Bill goes straight through to Secunderabad. I hear Wilkinson arriving.

Bidar 25-12-30

We arrived here by car yesterday from Utgir and Bill went in to Secunderabad and I follow tomorrow. We are occupying the rest house on the fort wall. It is a very pleasant spot with a deep verandah overlooking the plain with a cliff 300 feet high immediately below. It is so convenient for disposing of matches, cheroot ends, egg shells, orange peel and other refuse. Unfortunately the old Maharaja is coming here today and we have done him out of the rest house. I offered to vacate and return to Utgir but the Taluqdar would not hear of it and assured me that he would get into trouble with the Maharaja if we left. The Blairs arrived here with Miss Burney about noon yesterday and are living in the rest house. I occupy a tent nearby. I spent the morning exposing about 100 feet of film on the fort and street scenes. I have got a new filter for the camera. The Kodak people realized that they had made a mistake and sent the correct filter to Secunderabad. I shall be very interested to see what I have produced on these two reels.

We shot a buck on the way from Utgir – at least Bill did. He shot it with my rifle. I am not keen on killing things these days – particularly deer – but we wanted to make sure of Christmas dinner. I don't think we need have worried because the Blairs had two lorry loads of luggage – mostly food and bedding, as far as I could see. They have arranged for various people to visit them while they are here.

The Taluqdar and Police Superintendent of Bidar are very agreeable. They have been round twice to call and look after our wants. Unfortunately, Zain Yar Jung, the Taluqdar, does not speak English and our conversation is confined to essentials. They are cleaning up Bidar Fort and have removed a lot of cactus and rubbish since I was here a year ago. You can see now what the building was like and some tiled panels and stone carvings have been exposed. I fancy they may have trouble with the remaining walls because the rubbish helped to support them and with its removal there may be some collapse. The fortifications are well preserved. It is the buildings inside which are collapsing. I hope you will get a good idea of the place from the photographs.

Most Indian gateways have over them a few rooms and an alcove called the *nobut khana*, a sort of minstrels gallery. Three times a day, music is performed but I have no idea of the significance of the rite. The *nobut* is operating now, about five men with drums and a sort of flageolet. It is a pleasant sound in the distance and a picturesque sight at night. Lady Trench took me up to see it last time I was here.

I am posting this midday today to be certain of the English mail. There is only one daily train but it is well filled and the station presents a busy scene in the middle of the day. The buildings are inconspicuous and do not detract from the appearance of the place but it seems odd for a train to puff along round the side of the ancient walls."

So ends this instructive and entertaining account of a tour across a little known tract of the sub-continent. The cine film referred to still exists. It is in an early colour process and though not of first class quality, it helps to illustrate the scenes described.

Managing Director

It was in 1929 that negotiations began between the Nizam's Government and the Company for the takeover of the railway by the State. Some motive for this has already been suggested, namely, the desire of the Government to extend railway development for social and economic reasons quite apart from commercial justification. Already the State owned much of the permanent way, yet the bulk of the profits were earned on that part owned by the Company and although the State was entitled to a share of this profit, it did not seem altogether fair to it that the jam should go to the stockholders in Britain. One other factor that has not been mentioned was that the railway used coal mined in the state mines at favourable rates and this contributed to the handsome profit record of the Company. In a way, this was something of a present made by the State to the stockholders. Finally, it should be remembered that most of the major railways in British India were already state owned. That the Nizam's Government should wish to follow the trend cannot have come as too much of a surprise to the stockholders.

The negotiations were complex and lengthy and extended into 1930. Consultants were called in to make a valuation but Lloyd Jones was closely involved throughout. He was in a peculiar position. As Agent, he was still a servant, and a valued servant, of the Company. He was also a close personal friend of Sir Akbar Hydari and fully trusted by the Hyderabad Ministers. He had always fostered this dual loyalty as a result of which there had seldom been conflict between the Company and the State. Furthermore, he had fought stubbornly when the occasion arose for the interests of Hyderabad as against those of British India. It was not, in fact, uncommon for those working in India to place the interests of those they worked for before those of their own country. The result was that he was trusted by both parties and as he once put it, the whole negotiations rested in his own hands. At the final Company Meeting, the Chairman addressed the stockholders as follows "To Mr. Lloyd Jones' clear vision, striking personality and business ability I readily attribute the success of the negotiations with H.H.'s Government and on this account he merits special consideration. He has succeeded in making a good bargain for you as well as a good bargain for the State." It was a generous settlement, the stockholders receiving £ 300 for each £ 100 of stock. No doubt such terms were responsible for the business going through smoothly, especially as at this time the world slump was making itself felt and the price of the Company stock on the stock market would be on the decline.

From the point of view of the Nizam's Government, it was also a good bargain. They were acquiring a valuable asset and although the immediate prospects may not have been too favourable, the long term earning power of the railway was considerable. What, however, was their main concern was to have complete control over the communications system of the state. The only awkwardness over the negotiations did not concern the Company or Llyod Jones. Part payment to the stockholders was to be made in the form of Nizam's Government debentures and it was necessary that these be secured by the Government of India and the Bank of England. Conditions imposed by the latter were considered to be unduly onerous, which caused some bad feeling on the part of the Nizam's Government. One nice feature of the Company Meeting was the solicitude shown by stockholders for the railway staff. Some guarantee was demanded that the future employment of those who had worked faithfully for the company would be safeguarded under the new arrangement. In fact, the State guaranteed the same terms of service as before to all employees.

To the credit of the Nizam's Government the work of the London Board was fully appreciated as having substantially contributed to the successful running of the railway. It was therefore decided to continue the same system and a Board of Management was retained in London. It was reconstituted with Llyod Jones as Managing Director and Sir James Brunyate, retired from the Indian Civil Service, as Chairman. A condition of service was that Lloyd Jones should spend four months each year in Hyderabad and other directors should be prepared to visit India when required.

Something might be said here on the subject of honours. Lloyd Jones was awarded the C.I.E. (Companion of the Indian Empire) in 1925 for the work he had done for the Government of India. It was always felt by his friends that a *K* would be added in due course. Certainly the Hyderabad authorities pressed hard for this recognition for the services he had rendered to the State. Among Europeans in India a knighthood was normal for those who had attained certain positions in the services or had risen high in their professions and it was never understood why a career as distinguished as his should not be recognised. The simplest explanation is that the Agent of a State railway such as Hyderabad was not a post which according to protocol carried a knighthood with it and to make an exception in Lloyd Jones case would create a precedent. He claims that after the completion of the takeover negotiations of the railway a hint was dropped about accepting a knighthood. However, he was offhand in his response and nothing more was said. It is certainly true that he attached no importance to honours. The only thing that might have worried him was that the omission in his case was such that might almost amount to a mark of disfavour.

A big change now came in his mode of life. His headquarters were established in the United Kingdom and his domicile ceased to be in India. A house was bought in Guildford which became the family home and permanent residence. Kathleen remained the whole year in Guildford, looking after the two girls who went to school locally and the boys while on holiday. During most of the year, Lloyd Jones commuted up to London to attend office in the city. In addition, a continuous flow of visitors to the house meant an energetic and lively social life. These were mostly friends and colleagues from India, many of them being Indians.

Around November each year Llyod Jones set sail for India. He must have been one of the best customers of the P & O, although he sometimes varied the routine by going to Italy and travelling Lloyd Triestino. He used to tell the joke that the advantage of travelling by the Italian line was that if the ship sank, "There was none of that damned nonsense of 'women and children first'." He enjoyed his sea voyages as providing two to three weeks of comfortable leisure in an otherwise hectic existence.

In Secunderabad his situation had changed. No longer being Agent, he could not occupy the Agent's Bungalow. An old bungalow was renovated for the use of himself and the other directors when in India. A reference is made to the alterations to the bungalow towards the end of the Tour Diary. What was being done was the removal of the roof to the big centre room to make a sort of interior patio in the Spanish manner. It was a great success providing somewhere cool to sit in the evenings without the exposure of the usual open verandah. As we have seen in detail, Llyod Jones liked to spend as much time as possible out in the country on new line works or regular inspections. The new management pushed ahead vigorously, extending the railway and developing road services.

Being now a servant of the State, he spent more time than before in meeting the Indian gentry and attending official functions in Hyderabad. His assistance was also called for in matters unconnected with the railway. He presided over a commission to reorganize technical education in Hyderabad. He found that there was a tendency to encourage academic courses leading to a degree, for which there was little demand among employers and to neglect practical workshop training for which there was a demand. He also sat on an enquiry into an accident at the power station.

He still did work for the Government of India. In particular he worked on a scheme for improving the rates structure on the Indian railways. His early training on statistics came in useful here and he was able to show graphically how a comparatively small increase in fares could generate a disproportionate rise in profits. This was of interest to the Government of India who were always on the look out for means of raising additional revenue. Another important involvenemt was his appointment to a committee of railway experts in connection with the constitutional changes being negotiated at the Round Table Conferences. This brought him into distant contact with some of the political figures of the day and more closely with Sir Walter Monckton, the legal adviser to the Nizam's Government.

This full and pleasant life, combining the climatic ideal of a summer in England with a cold weather in India, continued through the thirties. His family was growing up and he was able to see more of them. He visited and was visited by his relations and friends in England and from his engagement books it is astonishing the amount of travelling that he got through during these years. In Britain, it was mostly by car at a time when motoring was still a pleasure. When journeying by train and ship, it was always in the maximum of comfort, a form of transport much slower than modern air travel but which had much to recommend it. He frequently met interesting people on these voyages, such as Lutyens on his way to build New Delhi or Keynes, busy advising the Government of India on the rupee exchange rate.

In the late thirties, with the children now independent, Kathleen was able to accompany her husband to India and she renewed her friendships in Secunderabad. On one visit the eldest daughter, Judy, who had grown into an attractive young lady, joined her parents and took part in the extensive social activities connected with the Nizam's Jubilee. Although much of the entertainment was lavish, at the Nizam's own banquet the food provided was recorded as being hardly what one would expect at the table of the richest man in the world, more to the standard of Jo Lyons Corner House. The Nizam went around in a Rolls Royce but it was 1914 vintage. The last visit of all to India was in the autumn of 1938, when Michael, the second son, accompanied his mother and father on his way to take up his appointment in the I.C.S. In the following year, war broke out and although Lloyd Jones did not give up all hope of going out again, it soon became impossible.

It was probably never intended that the London Board should be a permanent feature – rather an intermediate stage until the Hyderabadis felt confident of running the railway on their own. In any case, they had the assistance of a highly competent Agent in Colonel Slaughter. What brought the matter to a head was the difficulty of communication during war time. Lloyd Jones and the other directors were no longer able to fulfil their contracts to visit India and the postal services were often disrupted. So it was decided to transfer the entire management to an Indian Board and to close the London office. Llyod Jones was meticulous in handing over charge and wrote a detailed memorandum of the work before the London Board, which would require continued attention. The subjects extended from relations with the Government of India and with other railways, especially in regard to the constitutional changes that were taking place, to such matters as new line construction, finance, labour relations and road transport. This memorandum suggests that the London Board earned its keep.

The continued interests of Hyderabad and the railway in particular were represented by Lloyd Jones in a personal capacity. He maintained a small office in Guildford until the end of the war. He represented the Nizam's Government in various miscellaneous matters which cropped up. For example he was present when a cheque for £ 100,000 from the Nizam was handed over to the R.A.F. for the purchase of Spitfires.

In the early part of the war, Lloyd Jones undertook to act as Consulting Engineer for the Air Ministry to accelerate the installation of oil storage tanks. He was asked to undertake other tasks subsequently but felt that the work offered was outside his experience. He was content for the rest of the war to look after the interests of the Nizam's Government as well, perhaps with memories of his days in the Secunderabad Volunteers, serving as a private in the local Home Guard.

During his long retirement which lasted over thirty years, he remained in Guildford. He still saw many of his friends from India days, both British and Indian. The extensive pre-war entertaining had to be curtailed on account of lack of domestic staff and as he got older he felt less inclined to travel. He took an active part in local affairs, mostly of a charitable nature. He was on the Board of Governors of the Guildford Technical College, on the Income Tax Appeals Tribunal, and was Treasurer of the Surrey Boy Scouts and the Guildford Archaeological

Society. More as a recreation he also undertook book binding for the Red Cross.

However, what he really devoted himself to until he was in his late nineties, was the study of philosophy, religion, politics and economics. The year's sabbatical that he had enjoyed in 1911 had given him a grounding in some of these subjects and in addition he had a leaning towards abstract thought. He accompanied his reading with written critiques of what he had read and was always anxious to enter into lengthy and some times heated discussions with anyone of like interests. The parson got so embroiled in theological argument that he found it advisable to discontinue his visits. One subject that occupied much time was statistics. With his love of figures and his previous use of the method while in India, he developed a theoretical system, which he tried to interest certain academics in, but without success. The mass of papers which he diligently worked on remain to stupefy the present writer, innumerate as he is, with incomprehension.

Recognition of Llyod Jones' professional abilities was accorded in his election as fellow of the Institute of Civil Engineers and the City and Guilds Institute.

Kathleen, his wife, died in 1968 which caused him great grief. The marriage had been a happy one despite, some might say because of, lengthy separation. The deep love remained all their lives with nothing arising seriously to cloud their happiness. A sense of humour which they shared helped to iron out the slight irritations which inevitably occur in any marriage. Cyril always counted as the greatest blessing in his life, the love that existed between them. There was sorrow again at the death of his eldest son, Richard, in 1975. But living as he did into his hundredth year, the loss of loved ones and of his friends was inevitable. Nevertheless, his contentment and satisfaction with life survived until the end – cherished as he was by his surviving family and friends and cared for by his devoted housekeeper.

Conclusion

In concluding this memoir, it would be appropriate to make some estimate of the value of Cyril Lloyd Jones' life. In later life, he would concern himself with what he had contributed to the sum of human betterment. He was inclined to disparage his achievements. He undoubtedly regretted the disappearance of Hyderabad as a separate State of India. Without having any exaggerated estimate of the ability or integrity of the Hyderabadi ruling class (always excepting, of course, his great friend, Sir Akbar Hydari, who was not a Hyderabadi, in any case), he had great affection for the people and valued their independence and particular mode of life. In that it was archaic, it could not hope to survive but he was sad to see it go, nonetheless. He also received reports from time to time of deteriorating standards on the railway. After the Indian Independence, the Nizam's State Railway ceased to exist as such and was incorporated in a regrouping of all the Indian railways. Hence, what he regarded as his railway ceased to be a recognizable entity. It is inevitably sad to see something to which one has devoted one's life disintegrate, even when it is the result of historic change.

This depreciatory judgement was undoubtedly erroneous. The work of railway builders in India was of outstanding value. As a Government leader in India put it, "The railways are almost the greatest thing the British have done in India. I am not merely referring to the effect they have had in developing the country and in increasing its trade and industry and therefore its wealth. Nor am I referring to the fact that thanks to the railways, famines have largely lost their terrors in India. The material benefits which the railways have conferred on India are indeed great, but there are other benefits of a more intangible kind. We all know how much the railways have done to break down the barriers of caste and to promote unity among the peoples of this great continent."

One has only to read accounts of travel in India before the railways came, when it took about a month to go from Calcutta to Delhi, to understand what a revolution they brought. Moreover, travel became available for the masses, since, as has already been said, it was the cheapest form of mechanical transport ever devised. In opening up the country to improved agriculture and trade, railways were indeed decisive. This has all survived and may almost be said to be permanent. The wealthier Indian may now be able to fly and for short distances, cars and buses are now available. But more than in any other part of the world, railways are still used in India for the bulk of distance travel and for the transport of goods. The standards of management may not be what they were in Lloyd Jones's day but the railway lines, the bridges and stations are still there and the trains still run. He was prominent among that body of devoted men who established and developed the railway system for which the ordinary simple Indian has every reason to be grateful.

While the tangible achievements of Llyod Jones as an engineer are important and far more lasting than most men's life work, it was, perhaps, in the sphere of human relations that he was most significant. He was highly regarded by all who worked with him. Here is one among many testimonials – this from one of his engineers – "The longer I have been on the railway, the more I have seen and appreciated your work, not just the stuff of bricks and mortar, but ideas, valuable ideas of method and procedure, which represent the very solid foundations of sound administration." Through his superior ability he outstripped both his contemporaries and his seniors without rousing resentment or envy. His merits were so indisputable that most men were anxious to benefit from his example. This appreciation extended to both British and Indians. The surviving affection and regard with which he was held is shown by the volume of correspondence which continued for almost forty years after he left India. Here is an extract from a letter from the first Indian to be appointed General Manager of the Railway, J.N. Nanda, "I owe you a debt of gratitude for any success I may have achieved in my profession, as you were always a source of help and inspiration in my career."

With his abilities it is possible that had Llyod Jones' career developed in other directions, there might have been more in steel and concrete to show for it. His close friend Sir Ralph Freeman, who shared very similar qualities, was responsible for more noteworthy structures. Undoubtedly if Lloyd Jones had accepted one of the many opportunities to go to the United States, say, at a time of enormous expansion and development, he would have attained greater fame and material success. Yet he claimed that he had no regrets for staying where he did. To some degree, he might have felt selfish for having settled for a life which he really enjoyed and which, though to some extent restricted, gave him great satisfaction. Behind his feeling of lack of achievement might have lain the realization that his talents had not been allowed their full scope. Against this, if one looks at the benefits that he brought to the region where he had chosen to labour, no one need criticize him for not having cast his net wider.

III

The Nizam's State Railways: A Bibliographic Note

Omar Khalidi

The purpose of this note is to bring to the attention of scholars certain works that have a bearing on the development of railways in the Nizam's Dominions. Not consulted by any writer on the topic is E.M. Norie's *Military Reports on H.H. The Nizam's State Railway.* Madras, 1882. Salar Jang I's agent in London, John Seymour Keay (1839-1909) played an important role in securing loans for the railways. For an account of his life see the entry under his name in the (British) *Dictionary of National Biography: From the Earliest Times to 1900*. London: Oxford University Press, 1920. A brief introduction to the railway situation as it stood in the 1920s was written by Ethel Rosenthal. *His Exalted Highness the Nizam's Guaranteed State Railways. Asiatic Review* (London) 22 (1926): 578-588. In early 1930, Hyderabad state acquired all the assets and properties of the Nizam's State Railways, a comment on the acquisition is made by S. Keshava Iyengar in *The Hyderabad Railway Purchase: An Economist's Review* Hyderabad, n.d. A former manager of the railways, E.W. Slaughter, has described his account in "The Coordination of Road, Rail and Air Services in Hyderabad State: Experiences in the Field of British Transport Vehicles and Control of State-Owned Services under an Administration." *Journal of the Institute of Transport* (London) October-November 1947, pp. 554-558. Another manager, Syed Mahmood Alam wrote a brief account of his troubles with the Indian army when Nehru's tanks marched into Hyderabad in September 1948 in what was officially termed "Operation Polo", see the first chapter of Alam's work *Islam, Christianity and World Peace.* Manila: the Author, 1987.

Among the academic studies, pioneering work was done by Vasant Kumar Bawa, beginning with Salar Jang I and the Nizam's State Railways, 1860-1883. *Indian Economic and Social History Review* 2 (1965): 307-340. Two chapters in his book *The Nizam Between Mughals and British: Hyderabad State under Salar Jang I.* New Delhi: S. Chand, 1988., entitled "The Communication Network," pp. 90-100, and "The Financing of the Nizam's State Railways," pp. 117-128, deal with the subject under consideration. Along similar lines, Bharati Ray has also written a thesis presented to the University of Calcutta, later published as *Hyderabad and British Paramountcy, 1858–1883*. New Delhi: Oxford University Press, 1988, see chapter V, "The Introduction of Railways," pp. 132-164. Earlier a portion of Ray's thesis had been published as "The Genesis of Railway Development in Hyderabad State: A Case Study in the Nineteenth Century British Imperialism." *Indian Economic and Social History Review* 21 (1984): 45-69. An overview of the railway development during the reign of Mahbub Ali Khan is given in Sheela Raj's *Mediaevalism to Modernism: Socio-Economic and Cultural History of Hyderabad 1869-1911*. Bombay: Popular Prakashan, 1987, see pp. 145-75. Finally, Tara Sethia has written a dissertation at the University of California at Los Angeles in 1986 entitled "Railway and Mining Enterprises in Hyderabad State under the British Raj, during the 1870s and 1880s. Her conclusion: *Railway Construction and Mineral Exploitation* was developed and delayed according to the needs of the British government!

Index